BEING HAPPY!

written and illustrated by
Andrew Matthews

PRICE STERN SLOAN

Los Angeles

Being Happy
Copyright ©1990, 1988 by Andrew Matthews and Media Masters Pte. Ltd.

Published by Price Stern Sloan, Inc.
11150 Olympic Boulevard, Suite 650
Los Angeles, California 90064
Printed in Singapore by Grenadier Press.
1 0 9 8 7 6 5

Also by the same author: **MAKING FRIENDS**

This book has been printed on acid-free paper.

ISBN 0-8431-2868-2

ACKNOWLEDGEMENTS

To the many people who have helped me in my work and in the writing of this book, thank you. In particular, thank you to —

- my parents, Margaret and Peter Matthews, for always encouraging me in whatever I undertook
- those of you who have assisted with my seminars over the years — especially to Heather and Jerry Garreffa, Graeme Hoyle, Tereska Kropinski, Jacqueline Fong, Kristina Chionh and Julie and Kevin Manning.
- Chris Prior for your encouragement and belief in the book from the beginning
- Mary and Paul Blackburn, thank you for being such wonderful friends
- my sister, Jane Thomas, thank you for your ideas for the format of the book
- Shahreen Kamaluddin of Shahreen Corporate Communications, thank you for your advice and suggestions
- Norma and Ian Ward, thank you for editing and publishing *Being Happy*
- and Julie, to whom I dedicate this book, thank you for all of your love, support, and encouragement in helping me to experience "being happy" every day that we spend together.

CONTENTS

CHAPTER 1

PATTERNS

Life changes when we change.

PATTERNS

Let's take a look at this mind of yours. When you walk across the road, do you have to concentrate on every step? When you chew gum, do you have to think about it? When you eat a pizza, do you have to work at digesting it? ". . . now if I can just fix this anchovy, I can relax and go to sleep." When you go to sleep, do you need to concentrate to keep breathing?

You don't do any of these things with your conscious mind, do you? You do them with your subconscious. We might say that the mind is like an iceberg. There is the part we see, the conscious, and the much larger part we don't see, the subconscious. Our subconscious mind is responsible for a large slice of the results that we get in our life.

When we find history repeating itself in our lives, it is that part of our mind that is responsible. Many of us have recurring patterns — the same old experience or behavior keeps on cropping up.

Do you know somebody who is always late? I used to play tennis with a fellow who was always late. We would play tennis before work at the Hilton. I would say, "David, we are playing tennis tomorrow at 7:00 a.m." He would say, "I will be there." "Have you got that time?" "7:00 a.m. I will be there!"

Sure enough, at 7:15 next morning David would arrive. He had all the excuses. "My son had borrowed my racquet and put it under his bed." Next week, the same thing would happen. At 7:16 David would arrive. The reason: "I could only find one tennis shoe!" The following week, he arrived at 7:15 sharp. "The goldfish was sick and the baby was crying." And so on through the flat batteries, power failures, lost car keys and underwear that was left wet in the washing machine.

Finally, I said, "David, let's make a deal. For every minute that you are late from now on, it will cost you a dollar." He hurt his shoulder the next day and we have not played tennis since!

He thought that the world was doing it to him! He was not trying to be late consciously, but on his subconscious he had a program that said "you are always running behind" . . . and that program was running his life.

If David had accidentally got up early and found himself on target to arrive on time, his inner programs would have helped him find a tree to hit, or a strange road on which to get lost. He would have then taken a deep breath and said, "That's more like it — I am back behind the eight ball!"

". . . And then I caught the flu, the house burned down,
our car was stolen, George had to have an operation, the
cat got the flu . . ."

DRAMA PATTERNS. You probably know people who have drama patterns. Their lives are long dramas. You meet them in the street and make the fatal mistake of asking, "How are you?" You find out that the cat has just died, the car has been repossessed, Dad accidentally burned the house down, a meteorite wiped out their garage and they have just been diagnosed as having a very, very severe case of something that you have never heard of.

Whenever their life threatens to go smoothly, a little subconscious voice says, "Hey, this can't be right!" and very soon another drama emerges. They lose their job, they have another operation, they get arrested . . . and everything returns to normal.

We are going to look at what we can do about these patterns later, but for the moment, let us identify some more.

ACCIDENT PATTERNS. Some people have a talent for having accidents. They spend their lives falling off ladders, off bicycles, out of trees, getting electrocuted and having car accidents. I know an insurance agent in her early twenties who has owned five cars since her sixteenth birthday. She told me, "Every time I bought a new car, someone smashed into the back of me. After five of those accidents, I quit buying new cars for my own survival!"

SICKNESS PATTERNS. Do you know anybody with a sickness pattern? Some people get colds twice a year. Some people get sick everytime a big opportunity comes along. Some people get sick every Monday morning!

MESS PATTERNS. Some people are inclined towards mess. They don't consciously try and do it, but their pattern is so strong! Their desk is a mess, their files are a mess, their hair is a mess. You can come along and straighten everything out for them and within twenty minutes, their office, their bedroom, their car, their lunchbox, all look like they have been through a hurricane.

BROKE PATTERNS. Have you met someone who is always broke? It is not what we make, but what we do with what we make! People with a 'broke pattern' work on an automatic program. Whenever they get·any spare cash, they go looking for somewhere to get rid of it. As sure as you get an itch and scratch it, they'll get some money and . . . spend it. (For those of you who are in sales, take heart!). Mostly, they never realize what is happening! They figure it is the economy or the government or their salary that has got them into trouble. But you could double their salaries and they would still be broke! In fact, the reason why most people who win lotteries lose the lot, is that their inner pattern is saying, "All this money doesn't feel right. It doesn't fit. You'd better do something about this."

INDISPENSABLE PATTERNS. If you have the indispensable pattern, you absolutely know that within three minutes of your going on holidays, the office will be hit by lightning and the sales staff will all come down with the flu. If we have a pattern like this, our belief system and our attitude will help to create and perpetrate the situation. Whenever we leave, all hell breaks loose

JOB CHANGE PATTERNS. A fellow who was thinking of changing his job came to see me recently. He said, "My company is pulling me down, our products are inferior, and I can't pay the rent."
 I said, "How long have you been in this job?"
 He said two years.
 I said, "What about the job you had before that?"
 He said, "That one I had for about two years."
 "And the one before that?"
 "Two years."
 "And before that?"
 "About twenty four months!"
 I said, "Where is the problem — with you or the company?"
 He said, "With me!"
 I said, "If you are the problem, why change companies?"
 In the course of our conversation I told him about a friend who had five jobs in the past eleven months. I said, "As a matter of fact, I would bet everything I own that in a year's time she won't be in the same employ-ment." That afternoon she rang me to tell me that she had quit her job! My life savings would not have been at risk!

Now this lady tells me that she is deliriously happy — so it is not for us to question whether her pattern is good or bad. Simply, it is good to recognize that we operate on programs. We may have car and house and relationship patterns operating along similar lines.

There is another pattern. It is the "PEOPLE-ARE-NASTY-LIFE-IS-HORRIBLE-WHY-IS-THE-WORLD-DOING-THIS-TO-ME-I-WISH-I-WERE-DEAD!" PATTERN. Again, we tend to create our own circumstances. This one is really no fun!

The "I ONLY EVER HAVE JUST ENOUGH TO GET BY" PATTERN. In this one, our conscious and our subconscious thinking lock us in to a situation where life is a struggle but we always "get by."

Do you relate to any of these?

The "I ALWAYS MISS OUT" PATTERN. It manifests in our being born, starting school, buying businesses, going on vacation either too early or too late! Always being in the right place at the wrong time! Also, we may have the right talents but the wrong teachers or the right teachers but the wrong talent, or no teachers and no talent.

THE "PEOPLE ALWAYS RIP ME OFF" PATTERN. Need we say more?

e've started by looking at some negative patterns. There are, however, some very positive patterns, which you will relate to.

THE "I'M ALWAYS HEALTHY" PATTERN. Our state of health is determined by the programs we have between our ears which say who we are and what happens to us.

Do you know somebody who is "ALWAYS IN THE RIGHT PLACE AT THE RIGHT TIME?" They go into business just as the boom starts, they sell their house just before the factory is built next door, they go on holidays and bump into some millionaire who flies them around Europe. And you think, how do they do it? If I had just a quarter of their luck! Being in the right place at the right time is a pattern.

What about the "WHATEVER I DO, I ALWAYS END UP MAKING MONEY" PATTERN? Some people have it! Or the "Whatever I buy, I always get a good deal" pattern? (And the reverse of that is the "I always get a lemon pattern!")

Other patterns include the "I TRUST PEOPLE AND THEY ALWAYS TREAT ME WELL" program and the "WHATEVER I DO IS ALWAYS

FUN AND EASY" pattern.

We'll assume you want to hang on to the good patterns. What about the patterns you don't want? Thus we ask ourselves, "These rotten patterns I have — when will they change? When will they stop? **The answer is, "Life changes when we change!"**

CHANGE IS ALWAYS CHALLENGED

I t is not always easy to change our patterns, but it is very possible. Wherever you are, you can get to where you want to be, and we deal with how to do this throughout this book.

Recognize one thing right here. Whenever we decide to change, we meet resistance. We are always challenged to see if we are serious.

Let us assume that you decide to go on a diet. This is the big week in which you start shaving off your spare tire. This very week your mail box is stuffed with dinner invitations, cocktail party invitations, anniversaries. All change will be challenged, particularly in the beginning.

Let us say you make the decision that for the first time in your life you will open a savings account and begin to amass your personal fortune. You

cancel dinner at the Hyatt, which is part of your diet plan anyway, and you have your sixty three dollars earmarked for the bank. Isn't that just the day that your car insurance falls due, your refrigerator explodes and your brother-in-law needs the hundred dollars that you borrowed from him last Christmas?

Imagine you are used to dressing like a bit of a slob. Every time you put your best trousers on, you get them hopelessly dirty just by walking from the bedroom to the bathroom! Only, with your best trousers! Now the tendency is to think, "Well, that is the way I am. I can't change." The truth is that you can change, but the old patterns will try and persist.

So how do we change?

First, recognize that all change will be met with resistance. In a word, be prepared.

THE FORMATION OF PATTERNS

We begin to form behavioral patterns right from birth. Thus, they are persistent and tenacious.

For example, let's look at eating patterns. When we were babies, we cried for many different reasons: we were thirsty, hot, cold, lonely, frustrated, wanting a cuddle, exercising our lungs, wet, wanting a toy, wanting attention and so on. When we did cry, on many, many occasions, we were fed. Thus the association was formed that the solution to any of the above was to put something in our mouths. So if you smoke, drink or over-eat, you don't need to look very hard to see where some of your programing comes from.

When you are frustrated, lonely or depressed you know why one of the great lights in your life is the one in the refrigerator. The "solution" of the bottle and the cigarette stems, in part, from similiar conditioning.

For similar reasons, many of our other current characteristics result from early childhood experiences. In early years we are open-minded and empty-headed: we absorb information like a sponge. Since our first relationships are with our parents, their influence on our later lives and our later relationships is huge. Partly consciously and mainly subconsciously, we create patterns in our lives which reflect the experience we had with our parents. For example, we —
  * establish relationships with people who resemble our parents. For example, we may find ourselves working for bosses or establishing

friendships with people who resemble our mother or father.

* we establish relationships with other people that mirror our parents' relationships with others. If our parents were loving and gentle, so will we tend to be. If they spent time abusing people, we pick that up initially.

* we attract partners who resemble our mother or father. This we may do, not once or twice, but repeatedly. This can be because we form a subconscious picture from a young age that says, for example, "real men are tall and dark and silent" (like my Dad) or "a woman should be short and well mannered," (like my mother). Totally unaware of this on the conscious level, we may then go looking for the partner to fit the picture.

Also, the quality of our relationships with our parents creates its pattern. If, as children, we'd experienced guilt or disapproval then we will continue to attract and associate with people who treat us as "bad" people. Similarly, if we experienced love and approval as children, then, as adults, we will gravitate toward people who treat us with respect. In short, we attract what we expect and the world treats us as we believe we deserve to be treated.

"No way will I ever turn out like Father!"

We are only skimming the surface here. However, realizing that a problem recognized is a problem half solved, it is valuable to be aware of your patterns and have some idea of how they came about.

IN A NUTSHELL.

We are never stuck with patterns. Old negative patterns may be tenacious but they are not invincible. Always think positively about yourself and your condition. Mental discipline in this area may not be easy but the rewards are great. Always speak well of yourself and consistently visualize your life working as you want it. You will be creating new happiness patterns.

Listen to motivational cassettes and devour books on success. Use affirmations, subliminal tape programs and spend time with people from whom you can learn. You can rewrite your patterns to become what you choose.

In addition, use the "Nutshells" in this book to systematically shed the things from your life that bog you down, and consolidate the patterns that can push you ahead.

SELF-IMAGE

Have you ever noticed that when you are feeling good about yourself, other people become very nice? Isn't it funny how they change!

The world is a reflection of ourselves. When we hate ourselves, we hate everybody else. When we love being who we are, the rest of the world is wonderful.

Our self-image is the blueprint which determines exactly how we will behave, who we will mix with, what we will try and what we will avoid; our every thought and every action stem from the way we see ourselves.

The picture we have of ourselves is colored by our experiences, our successes and failures, the thoughts we have had about ourselves and other people's reactions to us. Believing this image to be fact, we proceed to live absolutely within the bounds of this picture.

Therefore, our self-image determines —

* how much we like the world and how much we like living in it
* exactly how much we will accomplish in life

We are what we believe we are. Hence, Dr. Maxwell Maltz, author of the bestseller "Psycho-Cybernetics" wrote, "The goal of any psycho-therapy is to change an individual's image of himself."

If you see yourself as being hopeless at mathematics, you will always have difficulty with figures. Perhaps sparked by some bad early experiences, you will have developed an attitude that says, "No matter what, I can't do math." Therefore, you don't try. Generally, you will fall further and further behind. If ever you do succeed, you say "It's a fluke." When you don't succeed, you say, "There! That proves I am hopeless!" Chances are that you would also tell others that you can't add up. The more you tell your brother and your husband and your neighbor and your bank manager that you are a hopeless case, the more you believe it, the more deeply embedded that self-image becomes.

The first step toward a vast improvement in our results is to change the way we think and talk about ourselves. A slow learner can begin to become a fast learner as soon as he changes his ideas about his own capabilities. If your self-image says that your co-ordination is excellent, you'll pick up new sports easily. If your self-image says you are a klutz, then you will spend so much time worrying about dropping the ball and succeeding in doing exactly that.

So long as you see yourself as someone who is always broke, you will remain broke. If you see yourself as a financial winner, you will be prosperous.

Our self-image is like a thermostat and we continue to perform within the prescribed range. It may be that Fred expects to be happy about fifty percent of the time. Therefore, whenever things are going extra well for Fred, he'll think, "Wait! Things aren't meant to be this good! Something is bound to go wrong any minute." When it does, Fred takes a deep breath and says, "I knew it couldn't last."

What Fred may not realize is that there are other people in the world who are unhappy all the time, and still others who are happy nearly all the time. We create our own quality of life, based on our own happiness self image.

What this means is that WE DECIDE on our own self-image. We decide on our own worth and decide how much happiness to expect.

COMPLIMENTS or, why not just say, Thank you . . .?

Our self-image determines our focus, or what we allow ourselves to think about. A good self-image allows us to concentrate on compliments paid to us and the successes we have achieved. This is not to be confused with having a big head. Someone once remarked, "Conceit is a weird disease. It makes everybody sick except the one that has got it!" *Being egotistical and having a healthy self-love are complete opposites.*

Being egotistical and having a healthy self-love are to be differentiated.

People with huge egos need to be the center of attention, crave recognition and have little concern for those around them.

On the other hand, a healthy self-love enables us to respect our own wishes as well as the wishes of others. It means we can feel proud of our

achievements without needing to broadcast them, and it means we can accept our shortcomings while striving to improve ourselves.

A healthy self-love means we have no compulsion to justify to ourselves or others why we take vacations, why we sleep late, why we buy new shoes, why we spoil ourselves from time to time. We feel comfortable doing things which add quality and beauty to life.

Let's recognize that there is no such thing as a "superiority complex."

When we genuinely appreciate our own worth, there is no need to tell the world how good we are. It is only the person who hasn't convinced himself of his own worth, who proceeds to inform the rest of humanity of his value.

Let's acknowledge that it is OK to accept a compliment when it is paid to us. We don't have to be perfect to accept a compliment with a graceful thank you. Successful people always do say, "Thank you". They realize that it is healthy to acknowledge a job well done.

If you congratulate Greg Norman on his winning a golf tournament, he won't say, "It was an accident." He won't say, "Just lucky". He will say, "Thank-you". If you were to congratulate Paul McCartney on a new hit record, he wouldn't say. "You're nuts! That record is junk." He would say, "Thank you." These men, like all successful individuals, have come to appreciate their own worth; and they did that long before they became successful, in order to be successful. As with any one of us, they needed to recognize their own value first.

A compliment is a gift. It takes thought and effort to bestow a compliment on somebody. Like any gift, it is disappointing to have it thrown back in your face. This is another reason to accept a compliment gracefully. Assume a friend of yours remarks on your striking appearance: to which you reply, "But I have got fat lips and short legs!"

Now you feel bad because you haven't accepted the compliment in the spirit in which it was given. They feel bad for the same reason, and remember you as their short-legged, fat-lipped little friend. Why not just say thank you?

THE "I" OTHER PEOPLE SEE

We can assess our own self-image by looking at the people around us. We form relationships with people who treat us the way we believe we deserve to be treated. People with healthy self-images demand to be respected by those close to them. They treat themselves well, and so set an example to other people as to how they should be treated.

If Mary has a bad self-image, she will put up with all kinds of garbage and abuse from just about everybody. In the back of her mind will be thoughts like, "I don't matter that much", "It's only me", and "I have always been treated badly. Perhaps I deserve it!"

We may ask, "How long will Mary have to put up with mistreatment?"

The answer is, "As long as she has a low opinion of herself."

People treat us the way we treat ourselves. Those with whom we associate quickly assess whether we respect ourselves. If we treat ourselves with respect, they will follow suit!

I imagine that we all know of women, with poor self-images, who have stumbled from one disastrous relationship to the next. Each time their partner has been a drunk or a "no-hoper". In each case they have found themselves being abused, either physically or emotionally. Unfortunately, the pattern will continue to repeat itself so long as they persist in their current self concept.

At the same time there are plenty of people who, having learned the hard way, have decided to expect and demand fair treatment from their friends, relatives and workmates. They have realized that when they made a stand, people responded.

YOUR WORTH

I magine that you were in charge of the care of a three-month old baby. At feeding time, would you feed the baby with no strings attached? Of course you would! You won't say, "OK kid! Unless you can do something smart or witty; unless you can sit up and say your ABCs or make me laugh, you don't get a drink!" You feed the baby because it deserves to be fed. It deserves love, care and fair treatment. It deserves all that because, like you, it is a human being, a part of the universe.

You deserve exactly the same. You deserved it when you were born and you deserve it now. Too many people get the idea that unless they are as clever or as smart or as handsome or as highly paid or as sporty or as witty as other people they know, they are undeserving of love and respect.

YOU DESERVE LOVE AND RESPECT JUST BECAUSE YOU ARE YOU.

Too rarely do most of us focus on our real inner beauty and our inner strengths. Do you recall watching "boy meets girl" movies? As the boy and girl struggled through thick and thin, you hoped and prayed the whole time that everything would work out. He went to war, she left home, he came back, she was gone, he found her, her brother told him to get lost, she told him to get lost, and all the time you hoped that they would live happily ever after. They were married and strolled off into the sunset as the curtain came down. You dried your tears and clutching your empty popcorn bucket, strolled out of the theater.

We cry at those movies because at our deepest level, we care. We love. We hurt. There is that inner core in all of us which is simply beautiful. Depending on how much we have been hurt, we will expose our deepest feelings, but we all share these qualities.

When we see the news stories which portray the plight of the starving around the globe, we all ache inside for them. Each of us may have a different view as to how they can best be helped, but we all care. That is the way we are.

Accept that you have these qualities — the capacity to love and empathize and be human. You are not *only human.* YOU ARE HUMAN. Recognize your own worth and constantly remind yourself that you deserve to be treated well!

THE STORY OF RAPUNZEL

Like many fairy stories, the tale of Rapunzel has a deeper meaning to it. It is a story about self-image. Rapunzel is a young lady who lives locked up in a castle, imprisoned by an old witch who continually tells her how ugly she is. One day, a handsome prince passes by the tower and tells Rapunzel of her loveliness. She lets down her golden locks, (apparently of some considerable length), so he may climb her hair to rescue her.

It is neither the castle nor the witch that has kept her a prisoner, but the belief in her own ugliness. When she recognizes her beauty, reflected in the face of her prince charming, she sees that she can be set free.

We all need to be aware of the witch or witches inside ourselves that are stopping us from breaking free.

SELF-IMAGE AND THE SUBCONSCIOUS

Our subconscious behaviour and our subconscious programs are intertwined with our self-concept. For example, when we are feeling badly about ourselves, we tend to take it out on ourselves. This may take the form of junk food binges, accidents, illnesses, overindulgence in alcohol or drugs, underindulgence in food and so on. This is not something that is necessarily a conscious act. It is simply that our treatment of ourselves will automatically reflect how much we like ourselves at any given moment.

There is even evidence to suggest that people who have car accidents are often feeling badly about themselves at the time, and that the accident is partly a subconscious punishment.

It is of prime importance that we do all in our power to keep thinking positive thoughts. This will ensure that we can stay happy people.

A bad self-image says. "I don't deserve". This leads to a person subconsciously sabotaging his/her own happiness. Whenever exciting opportunities come along, a chance to take a holiday arises or a chance to learn a new skill presents itself, that person will either consciously or subconsciously find reasons why it can't be done.

POOR SELF-IMAGE BEHAVIOR

ach of us must work continually on maintaining our positive and healthy self-image. The following behavior traits are evidence that there is room for improvement in our self image —
* jealousy
* negative talk about ourselves
* experiencing guilt
* failure to give compliments
* non-acceptance of compliments
* not taking our own needs into account
* not asking for what we want
* starving ourselves of luxuries unnecessarily
* failure to give affection
* inability to receive and enjoy affection
* criticism of others
* comparison of ourselves with others
* constant poor health

Change is difficult. The action of a poor self-image is always to perpetuate itself. As we start out on the road to self-improvement, the tendency is to keep replaying the old patterns of blame, guilt and self denigration. Here are some suggestions for things that you can do to boost the way you feel about yourself —
* ACCEPT COMPLIMENTS — always say thank you or words to that effect.
* GIVE COMPLIMENTS — one of the easiest ways to feel good about

ourselves is to recognize the beauty in others.

* ALWAYS SPEAK WELL OF YOURSELF — If you have nothing good to say about yourself, keep your mouth shut!
* PRAISE YOURSELF — when you do something right, give yourself a pat on the back. Acknowledge your value.
* SEPARATE YOUR BEHAVIOR FROM YOURSELF — realize that your behavior is not connected to your self-worth. If you do something silly, like smash into another person's car, it doesn't make you a bad person. You simply made a mistake. (Love the sinner, hate the sin).
* TREAT YOUR BODY WELL — it is the only one you have got. Everything we do affects everything else. Exercise and nourish it well.
* LET PEOPLE KNOW HOW YOU EXPECT TO BE TREATED — in particular, set an example by the way you treat yourself and them. Nobody should accept abuse from anybody!
* GET AROUND GOOD PEOPLE
* WORK AT HAVING PLEASURE WITHOUT GUILT * USE AFFIRMATIONS
* READ BOOKS WHICH GIVE YOU IDEAS AND INSPIRATION
* ALWAYS PICTURE IN YOUR MIND HOW YOU WANT TO BE, NOT HOW YOU ARE. YOU WILL THEN NECESSARILY GRAVITATE TOWARD YOUR DOMINANT THOUGHTS.

LOVE YOUR NEIGHBOR AS YOURSELF

L oving our neighbor as ourselves automatically assumes that we should love ourselves. Note that the instruction is not to run yourself down and build up your neighbor. We are not advised to deprive ourselves, to suffer and be miserable. My interpretation of "love your neighbor as yourself" is that we should maintain a balance between our needs and our neighbor's needs; respect both parties.

FALSE MODESTY

Perhaps you know people who extract compliments from others using reverse psychology. The conversation runs this way:

They say, "I'm a hopeless piano player!"

So you say, "I think you're very good."

They say, "Not really. I make lots of mistakes."

So you say, "It sounds great to me."

They say, "You're just being nice."

You say, "I mean it. You're fantastic!"

They say, "Thanks . . . but I'm really terrible."

Isn't this exasperating? We owe it to ourselves to end these ridiculous conversations as quickly as possible, and start talking about something sensible!

Exceptional people don't use false modesty tricks. They don't go fishing for compliments and they accept compliments gracefully when they are given.

HEALTH.

Scientific experiments have demonstrated incredible ways to kill guinea pigs. Emotional upsets generate powerful and lethal toxins. Blood samples taken from persons experiencing intense fear or anger when injected into guinea pigs have killed them in less than two minutes. Imagine what these toxins can do to your own body.

Every thought that you have affects your body chemistry within a split second. Remember how you feel when you are barrelling down the highway and a big truck suddenly brakes twenty meters in front of you. A shock wave shoots through your whole system. Your mind produces instant reactions in your body.

The toxins that fear, anger, frustration and stress produce not only kill guinea pigs but kill us off in a similar manner. It is impossible to be fearful, anxious, irritated and healthy at the same time. It is not just difficult, it is impossible. Simply put, your body's health is a reflection of your mental health. Sickness will often then be a result of unresolved inner conflicts which in time show up in the body.

It is also fascinating how our subconscious mind shapes our health. Do you recall falling sick on a day when you didn't want to go to school?

Headaches brought on by fear? Do you know anyone who got laryngitis before his big speech? The mind-body connection is such that if, for example, we want to avoid something, very often our subconscious mind will arrange it. Once we recognize that these things happen to us, we are half way to doing something about them.

Our belief system and our expectations can keep us sick. If our brother-in-law says, "I've got this rotten cold and you'll probably get it and be in bed for two weeks," then we become susceptible to the illness. We get sick in part because we expect it.

There is also evidence to suggest that we may suffer a disease because our parents had it and we think it is "appropriate" or inevitable. We carry subconscious patterns or programs around on our brain cells that keep us either healthy or sick. Some people say "I never get colds" and never get them. Others say "I always get at least two colds per year" and they succeed. This is not coincidence.

As children, we learn quickly that being sick is one of the most effective ways of getting attention. For some of us it is the only way. When we become sick, our friends and family rally around and immediately we feel more loved and reassured. Some people never break this pattern and for a lifetime manage to fall ill, fall off ladders and break legs whenever they feel ignored or unloved. Clearly, this is much more an unconscious than a conscious behavior. However, the fact remains that those people who feel loved and secure have far less illness and "accidents" than those

who don't.

Repressed feelings and emotions affect our health. The classic victim syndrome, "Don't worry about me. I'm not important" or "I'm used to being ignored and disappointed" or "I'll just sit here with a smile on my face and stew inside" is the beginning of disaster. To be healthy and energetic, we must maintain positive emotions and we must be expressing our feelings. It is also very important to believe we DESERVE to be healthy. If we harbor any subconscious feelings like, "I'm not a nice person" or "I've done a lot of bad things" or "I deserve to be punished", then a classic way to suffer is through ill health — sometimes for a lifetime.

If we are not doing the job or leading the life we enjoy, our mind is constantly holding the thought, "I wish I wasn't here." As our body is a slave of the mind, our body will then start getting us out of whatever we want to get out of. The first step is illness. The more permanent solution is death.

I don't suggest that our health can be totally explained by the preceding paragraphs. I do wish to emphasise the mental role in our physical health. If I take a banana to the South Pole, dig a hole and plant it, and, ten years later, return with a big basket to harvest my banana crop, how many bananas will I get? You say not very many? The reason is that the environment is bad for growing bananas. Well, through your thoughts and emotions you control your bodily environment. It is your choice whether you make it a hot house for germs or a temple of health.

Good health is your birthright; and by good health I mean energy and vitality. It is your right to wake each morning with the confidence that your body can more than just "struggle through." Too many people have the notion that good health means a mere absence of disease.

If we look at the mind — body connection, it is easy to see how much our body is affected by our mental state. Our subconscious mind is monitoring our healing processes every second of the day. Your body is continually rebuilding and its rebuilding blueprint comes from your mind.

When your wounded finger heals, what controls the binding of the new cells? What intelligence is it that ensures that when you lose a finger nail, it is another finger nail you grow on the end of your finger, and not a bladder? Something has to be controlling all these things! Let us not take the miracle of our physical being for granted!

Your mind is the architect of your body and your body is a reflection of your thoughts. If you are consumed by fear and anger and un-expressed emotion, your body will reflect it. The "disease" of the mind becomes "disease" in the body.

IN A NUTSHELL.

Think healthy, happy thoughts. Imagine yourself as healthy. Decide that good health is your birthright and that you deserve to be healthy. Above all, be gentle on yourself. Accept and love yourself where you are right now and acknowledge that even up until now you have been living life the best way you know how.

PAIN

hile we are on the subject of health, let's take a look at pain.

If you wander up to John Brown after he has spent an hour and a half with his dentist and remark, "Isn't pain wonderful?" John may suspect that you're a little crazy. Similarly, after you have burnt your fingers on the kitchen stove it may be difficult for you to appreciate how positive pain is.

But let us assume that you felt no pain. You could then absent-mindedly lean on that hotplate for twenty minutes until you casually turn around to see that where you once had an arm, you now have a charred, black looking stick. If you didn't feel physical pain, you could get home from work and bending down to put your slippers on, say to yourself, "Wow! Half of my left foot is missing. I must have chopped it off somewhere. Did I jam it in the elevator door or has this something to do with my neighbor's Doberman? I thought I was walking a bit strange this afternoon."

Physical pain has its valid, positive point. It is continual feedback to tell us what to do and what not to do. How embarassing it would be to have to explain in the middle of a romantic candlelight dinner, "I can't eat my dessert, darling. I just bit my tongue off." (The explanation in sign language, of course).

Whenever we eat too much or we don't get enough sleep or a part of our body is getting worn out or something is broken and needs a rest, our marvellous automatic alarm system lets us know.

Our experience of emotional pain operates along the same lines. If we are hurting emotionally, it is a message that we need to change our approach or see things differently. If we feel hurt, let down or dumped by someone in our life, the message may be, "Love those in your life without expectations. Accept them as they are and take what they want to give without judgement." Alternatively, the message may be, "Don't let the actions of others destroy your own self-esteem."

If your house burns down or someone steals your car, you may well experience emotional upset. This is normal and human. If you choose to learn from the situation you may well discover that you can live happily without the things to which you were so attached. The emotional upset may cause you to re-assess your priorities. I don't mean to say that we should live without houses and cars. I make the point that successful people learn from such experiences and adjust their values so life's hiccups become less painful.

IN A NUTSHELL

Pain causes us to contemplate: to change direction. It prompts us to look at things differently. With emotional pain as with physical pain, if we keep doing something stupid we keep getting hurt. We might say, "Well it shouldn't hurt, I don't want it to hurt," but it will still hurt. Some people manage to hurt over something twenty four hours a day, three hundred and sixty five days a year. They never realize it is time to take their hand off the stove.

WE BECOME A PART OF OUR EVERYDAY WORLD

We are very susceptible to the influence of the people around us. You may have known somebody who has gone overseas for a year or so, and has returned with an accent? Have you known any charming little five-year-olds who toddled off to school innocent and naive, and in no time at all, they learned more swear words than your average trooper?

We become a part of our immediate environment. None of us are immune to the influences of our own world — our friends, our family, our

workmates, the TV, the newspaper, the radio, the books and magazines we read. Let us not kid ourselves that we are untouched by the things and the people in our life. Our thoughts and our feelings, our goals and our actions are constantly being shaped by those and what we live with.

Fred goes off to his new job at the factory. Fred takes his ten-minute coffee break, the other workers take a half an hour. Fred says, "What is the matter with you guys?"

Two weeks later, Fred is taking twenty-minute breaks.

A month later, Fred takes his half hour. Fred is saying, "If you can't beat them, join them. Why should I work any harder than the next guy?"

Ten years later, Fred is taking the longest coffee break in the factory. He has adopted the attitudes of his co-workers.

The fascinating thing about being human is that generally we are unaware that there are changes taking place in our psyche. It is like returning to the city smog after some weeks in the fresh air. Only then do we realize that we have become accustomed to the nasty smells.

Mix with critical people and we learn to criticize. Mix with happy people and we learn about happiness. Mix with messy people and our lives become messy. Mix with enthusiastic people and we become enthusiastic. Adventurous people help us to become adventurous and prosperous people inspire us to be prosperous.

What this means is that we need to decide what we want from life and then choose our company accordingly. You may well say, "That is going to take some effort. It may not be comfortable. I may offend some of my present company." Right! But it is your life!

Fred may say, "I'm always broke, frequently depressed, have a boring job, I'm often sick, I'm going nowhere and I never do anything exciting." Then we discover that Fred's best friends are always broke, frequently depressed, hold boring jobs, often ill, going nowhere and wishing that life was more exciting. This is not coincidence. Nor is it our business to stand in judgement of Fred. However, if Fred ever wants to improve his quality of life, the first thing he will need to do is to recognize what has been going on all these years.

It is no surprise that doctors as a profession suffer a lot of ill health because they spend their lives around sick people. Psychiatrists have a high incidence of suicide in their profession for related reasons. Traditionally, nine out of ten children whose parents smoke, smoke themselves. Obesity is in part an environmental problem. Poor people have poor friends. Rich people have rich friends. Successful people have successful friends. And so the story goes on.

IN A NUTSHELL

IF YOU ARE SERIOUS ABOUT CHANGING YOUR LIFE, GET SERIOUS ABOUT CHANGING WHAT SURROUNDS YOU.

PROSPERITY

"The best thing you can do for the poor is not be one of them."

My experience has been that many people believe that when it comes to money and prosperity, all the positive thinking, hard work and right attitudes will never make a scrap of difference to their ability to pay the bills at the end of the month.

The fact is that your conscious and your subconscious thoughts are always creating results in your life INCLUDING determining how much money you have in the bank. Your prosperity or lack of it is a result of your thinking. Your mind and your belief system are what hold you right where you are, and your mind will keep you rich or poor depending on how you train it. What you think is what you get. Think poor, stay poor. Think rich, stay rich.

Let us take our friend Fred who believes that he will always be struggling to pay the bills. Fred will probably only apply for jobs which are relatively low paid positions because that is where he figures he belongs. He may very well only mix with people who are in his economic bracket because that is where he feels comfortable. These people confirm his ideas that life is tough. With such company, he will tend not to expand his ideas as to what is possible for him.

Chances are that Fred will have come from a family who has similiar attitudes to money and the inevitability of the lack of it. This will contribute to Fred's belief system.

As we get from life largely what we expect, and Fred expects to be short of cash, that is what he will get. Because he has a "program" on his brain cells which says, "You never have any money, Fred," he will probably find that every time he gets some spare cash, he will go out and spend it. Subconsciously he will think, "This feels a bit strange; having spare money like this! I had better buy something and get myself back to my normal state. — broke!"

Through his self-talk Fred will also confirm that money problems are a necessary part of life. He may say to himself, "I'll never have any money because I never got a good education." If good education was important in getting rich, university professors would probably all be millionaires. I know of many highly educated people who are always broke, and many people of little education who are incredibly wealthy.

Fred may reason, "I've got the wrong job to become wealthy." Well, many people get themselves a sideline in order to get a start. Others change jobs.

Time may be the key. Fred may reason that he doesn't have enough time to get wealthy. Well Fred, we each have all the time there is. That is twenty four hours in every day — nobody gets any more or any less.

Fred may say that he is too young or too old or that he has a wife to think of or that he doesn't have a wife to support him or that he has too many kids . . . Yet if he looks closely, he will see people creating their own financial prosperity while dealing with any combination of the mentioned factors.

Furthermore, our friend may argue that he would like to be prosperous but that he does not want to work himself into the ground. Again, we can find thousands of people who work long hours and stay poor. Equally, there are many who work respectable hours and get rich. Hard work is an ingredient, but it doesn't guarantee wealth! If you have your head down plucking chickens in a factory ten hours a day, plucking more chickens won't make you much better off. At some stage what you will need is a change of strategy!

I am making no judgements here. Money is neither good nor bad. Money is just money. Fred, or anybody else for that matter, may be perfectly happy as he is. The point is, though, that Fred's circumstances are self-created. If he ever decides to change, he can achieve his goals.

Shortly we will look at some action which Fred, (or you), could take to get wealthy.

MONEY BLOCKS

Let us look at how and why some people keep themselves from becoming wealthy.

Many people are uncomfortable with money for various reasons and hence they keep themselves poor. This may sound crazy but it is true. Imagine yourself in the following situations to see how comfortable you are about having money.

Situation A

You have just been to the bank and collected $5000 in cash to buy a second hand car. On the way home from the bank you meet a friend and stop for a coffee. While you are paying for the drinks, your friend notices that you have a wallet stuffed full of money.

Would you be embarrassed and hastily explain to your friend why you have so much money, or would you feel perfectly comfortable in carrying the money and explain nothing?

(IN ORDER TO MAKE MONEY OR SAVE IT, YOU NEED TO BE COMFORTABLE WITH IT. If you are uncomfortable with it, you will subconsciously, if not consciously, arrange for you to end up not having it.)

Situation B

You meet somebody at a party who matter-of-factly mentions, without boasting, that money is so easy to make he has it coming out his ears. How do you feel about the person and the comment?

(TO BE WEALTHY, WE NEED TO FEEL GOOD ABOUT OTHER PEOPLE BEING PROSPEROUS. If you have any deep-seated ideas that rich people are not nice, then you will keep yourself poor because you would not want to hate yourself, would you?)

Situation C

You are out shopping with a friend and you find that you have left all of your money at home. Your friend has sufficient to loan you some cash for the afternoon. How would you feel about asking to borrow fifty dollars? Would you prefer to go back home and pick up your own money?

(It is important for your own prosperity that you feel that you are worth helping out. IT IS IMPORTANT THAT YOU FEEL YOU DESERVE HELP, (AND MONEY) AS YOUR ABILITY TO RECEIVE DETERMINES YOUR PROSPERITY.)

Situation D

You put your hand in your pocket to find that you have just lost a hundred and twenty dollars. Do you say to yourself, "Oh well, somebody else probably needs it more than I do," or do you put yourself through hell for the next month for having lost the rent?

(IF WE ARE TOO ATTACHED TO MONEY IT BECOMES DIFFICULT TO MAKE IT AND DIFFICULT TO HANG ON TO IT.)

Situation E

Imagine that you are making more money in a month than your father makes in a year. How would you feel about that? Would you feel "guilty" for doing so well? How would you feel about him knowing that you are doing so well?

(IF SUCCESS IS AWKWARD FOR YOU TO DEAL WITH, YOU WILL BE HOLDING YOURSELF BACK FROM SUCCESS.)

Situation F

Many people associate poverty with spirituality. Their idea is that it is virtuous to be poor.

How do you think God would feel, on finding out that you are making half a million dollars per year? Do you think he would say, "What a greedy pig!", or do you think He would say, "Good luck to you! You must be doing something right."

PROSPERITY AND FREEDOM FROM WANT DEMONSTRATE THAT WE ARE BALANCED AS INDIVIDUALS. The spiritual texts encourage us to give to the poor, not join them in their poverty.

WHAT CAN I DO?

Here is a brief list of some things you can do to improve your financial situation.

1. DECIDE TO BE PROSPEROUS AND COMMIT YOURSELF TO PUTTING IN THE NECESSARY EFFORT. I want to emphasize that effort is very important, but it must be in combination with the right attitude and belief system.

2. SAVE FIRST AND SPEND WHAT IS LEFT. Poor people do the opposite. They spend first and figure they will save later. Wealth is largely a

matter of having a plan, and then sticking to it.

3. OBSERVE WEALTHY PEOPLE. Spend some time around someone who is doing well. Find out what the difference is between you and him. Pick out the positive, attractive points. Be objective. Study the qualities and the traits that make him tick. Watch him closely. Examine his attitudes and let these rub off on you.

4. ASK FOR SOME HELP. You may be surprised how much people are prepared to help you when they see that you are serious about helping yourself. Knowing how to ask for help aids our ability to receive.

5. CONSTANTLY RE-AFFIRM TO YOURSELF THAT YOU DESERVE TO BE PROSPEROUS.

6. SPOIL YOURSELF OCCASIONALLY. A part of the process of becoming financially independent is realising that you can afford to spoil yourself. Also, as you enjoy the money you have, you gain incentive to make more.

7. MAKE PLANS AND SET GOALS.

8. CONTINUALLY STRETCH YOUR BELIEF SYSTEM AS TO WHAT IS POSSIBLE FOR YOU TO ACHIEVE. There are hundreds of books and tapes available on personal success. If you get one good idea from a book or a tape, then the time and money spent was worth it.

9. ALWAYS CARRY SOME MONEY — FOR THREE REASONS. Firstly, you will feel more prosperous. Secondly you will get used to having money. Thirdly, you will learn to trust yourself with money. Also, you may eliminate fears you have about losing money, which is important for your prosperity.

SOME PEOPLE SAY, "I CAN'T CARRY ANY MONEY OR I'LL SPEND IT!" Well, how can they ever hope to have any money while they don't trust themselves with it?

10. DON'T BLAME YOUR PARENTS, THE WEATHER, THE ECONOMY, THE GOVERNMENT, YOUR JOB, YOUR EDUCATION OR YOUR MOTHER-IN-LAW FOR HOW YOU ARE DOING.

11. ATTACK EVERY CHALLENGE WITH ENTHUSIASM AND COMMITMENT. It is ironic that most wealthy peple find that they did not start really making money until they stopped working for it.

12. RECOGNIZE THAT POVERTY IS A MENTAL DISEASE. Like many diseases, it is curable for those who believe it can be cured. As with illness, it takes effort, initiative and courage to beat it — and if you give up, you're in trouble!

It is exciting to recognize that nearly all happy and prosperous people have beaten the disease at some time in their life. You can too!

CHAPTER 2

LIVING IN THE NOW

The present is all we've got.

LIVE, NOW!

All you have is **now.** The measure of our peace of mind and the measure of our personal effectiveness are determined by much we are able to live in the present moment. Regardless of what happened yesterday and what might happen tomorrow, NOW is where you are. From this point of view, the key to happiness and contentment must be in focusing our minds on the present moment!

One of the beautiful things about young children is that they absorb themselves totally in the present moment. They manage to stay totally involved in whatever they are doing, whether it be watching a beetle, drawing a picture, building a sandcastle or whatever else they choose to devote their energies to.

As we become adults, many of us learn the art of thinking about and worrying about several things at once. We can allow past problems and future concerns to crowd into our present such that we become miserable and ineffective.

We also learn to postpone our pleasures and our happiness, often developing a notion that sometime in the future everything will be much better than it is now.

The high school student thinks, "When I'm out of this school and don't have to do what I am told, then everything will be great!" He leaves school and suddenly recognizes that he won't be happy until he has left home. He leaves home and starts university and soon decides, "When I have got my degree, then I'll be really happy!" Eventually he gets his degree at which time he realizes that he can't be happy until he has a job.

He gets his job and has to start at the bottom of the heap. You guessed it. He can't be happy yet. As the years roll by, he postpones his happiness and peace of mind until he gets engaged, gets married, starts buying a home, gets a better job, starts a family, gets the kids in school, owns his home, gets the kids out of school, retires . . . and he drops dead before he allows himself to be blissfully happy. All his present moments were spent planning for a wonderful future which never arrived.

Do you relate at all to this kind of story? Do you know of anybody who has been putting off being happy until some time in the future? The thing about being happy is that you are mostly involved with the present. We decide to be happy on the journey, not just when we reach our destination.

Similarly, we can postpone spending time with the people who mean the most to us. A study was carried out some years ago in the United States where the object was to determine how much quality time middle class fathers spent with their young children. The participants had microphones attached to their shirts to monitor how much communication took place between father and child each day.

The study showed that the average middle class father spent about thirty seven seconds quality time per day with his child. No doubt many of the fathers involved had great plans for spending time with their loved ones "when the house is finished", "when the pressure is off at work", "when there is more money in the bank" . . . *The point is that None of us has a guarantee that we will be here tomorrow. Now is all we have got.*

Living in the now also means that we enjoy whatever we are doing for its own sake, and not just for the end result. If you happen to be painting your front verandah, you can make a point of enjoying every stroke of the brush, of learning everything there is to know about how best to do the job, all the while being aware of the breeze on your face, the birds singing in the trees and everything else that is happening around you.

Living in the now is about expanding our awareness to make the current moment more delicious rather than shutting off. Each of us has the choice, moment by moment, as to whether we really live and absorb and allow ourselves to be touched and affected.

Whenever we are living in the present moment, we drive fear from our mind. Essentially, fear is concern over events which might happen sometime in the future. This concern can be paralyzing to the point where we find it almost impossible to do anything constructive.

However, you are only open to intense fear when you are being inactive. The minute you start to take action and actually DO SOMETHING, fear subsides. Living in the now is about taking action without fear of the consequences. It is about putting in the effort for the sake of the involvement, without worry as to whether we will get our just rewards.

It is worthwhile remembering that we cannot replace a something with a nothing. If you have worries on your mind; such as your car has blown up or you have lost your job or your wife has left you, it is no easy matter to just empty out your mind and find peace. The easiest way to improve your mental state is to take action, get involved, participate. DO SOMETHING! ANYTHING.

Ring an old friend or make a new one, go to the gym, take the children to the park or help your neighbor in the garden.

IN A NUTSHELL

Time doesn't really exist, except as an abstract concept in your head. The present moment is the only time you have. Make something of this moment!

Mark Twain once remarked that he had been through some terrible things in his life, some of which actually happened! Isn't this so true? Our tendency can be to put ourselves through hell in our mind, contemplating what could come to pass, yet if we look at the present moment, which is all we have, there is no great problem at all!

Live in the now.

WAITING FOR THINGS

Have you ever noticed that when you are just sitting waiting for a taxi, it never seems to arrive? The same seems to be true for other things that we wait for. Hence the old saying, "A watched pot never boils".

Similarly, you may have found yourself waiting too long for a phone call sometime. After waiting for what seemed like hours, you decided to busy yourself with something else, and bingo! The call came through.

Whenever we sit and wait for letters, people, the right job, the perfect partner, some wonderful adventure, our entree in a restaurant, Christmas, or anything else we want, it takes a long time arriving. Sometimes it never comes.

There is a principle operating here which is telling us, "Get on and live your life in the present moment and don't hold your breath for things to happen." If we say to ourselves, "I must have "A" in order that I can be happy and fulfilled," then circumstances may very well arrange themselves to prove otherwise.

IN A NUTSHELL

Jump into life at every opportunity. Live in the now. While you are waiting for one thing to happen, do something else. If you are waiting for Hollywood to discover your prodigious talents, go take a class in basket weaving in the meantime! If your boyfriend is late in picking you up for the ball, read or organize your photo album or bake a cake until he arrives.

In doing so, you demonstrate a certain detachment from the end result.

"LETTING GO" OF THE SITUATION ACCELERATES RESULTS.

FORGIVENESS

T he decision to forgive yourself or somebody else is a vote to live in the present moment.

"I'll never forgive my mother for that!"

"I can't forgive myself!"

Are these familiar expressions? If we refuse to forgive somebody, then we are really saying, "Instead of taking some action to improve matters, I prefer to live in the past, and blame somebody for it. (or blame myself)." When we won't forgive ourselves, we are actually choosing to stay on a guilt trip so we can put ourselves through some extra mental anguish.

FORGIVING OTHERS

Some people seem to have forgiveness figured out backwards. They think that if they won't forgive their mother for being nasty, it is their mother's problem. It is not their mothers' problem; it is theirs! When we withhold forgiveness, WE suffer. Half of the time, the "guilty" person doesn't even know what is going on in our head! The "guilty" party continues to happily breeze through life while we put ourselves through so much mental anguish.

If I refuse to forgive my brother-in-law for not inviting me to his Christmas party, I suffer. He doesn't get the ulcers, he doesn't lose the sleep, he isn't upset, he doesn't get the nasty taste in his mouth. I do. It is no wonder that we are advised to "forgive those who trespass against us!" It is the only way we can remain happy and healthy. Unforgiveness is one of the greatest causes of sickness because a sour mind creates a sour body.

In addition, so long as we hold other people as being guilty and responsible for our unhappiness, we are refusing to admit to our own responsibility. Blaming other people never got anyone anywhere. The moment we stop blaming others, we are in a position to take some action to improve things. Blaming is an excuse to do nothing about reality — an excuse not to take action.

Fred might say, "I'll forgive you, but I can't forget". Fred is really saying, "I'll forgive you a little bit, but I want to hang on to some of this stuff just in case it is convenient to remind you about it later on." Real forgiveness is letting go.

I believe it is important to realize we all live our lives the best way we know how. We make a lot of mistakes along the way, sometimes we act on misinformation, sometimes we do stupid things, yet we are still doing it the best way we know. Nobody opens his eyes the moment he is born and thinks, "Great! Here is my big chance to go out and screw up my life!"

Our parents brought us up the best way they knew how. Based on the information they had, and the example that was set for them, they ventured forth into the unknown territory known as "parenthood". To blame them endlessly for a lousy job of parenting is fruitless and destructive.

Some people never forgive their parents and screw up their lives just to demonstrate to their parents what a lousy job they did! Their message is, "It is your fault that I am broke and lonely and unhappy so now you can watch me suffer!"

Blaming others gets us nowhere. If something is done, it is done. Griping about it changes nothing. Blaming the weather never helped anybody. The same goes for blaming other people.

When we do choose to forgive, a marvellous principle comes into operation. As we change, others change. As we alter our attitude toward others, they begin to alter their behavior. Somehow, the moment we choose to change the way we see things, others respond to our changed expectations.

FORGIVING OURSELVES

If forgiving others is difficult, forgiving ourselves is even harder. Many people spend their whole lives punishing themselves mentally and physically for what they believe to be their own shortcomings. Some over-eat, some under eat, some drink themselves into oblivion, some systematically destroy all their relationships, some live a life of poverty or sickness. At the root of this suffering can be a belief system which says, "I have done a lot of naughty things", "I am guilty", or "I don't deserve to be healthy and happy". You may be surprised at how many sick people there are who are not convinced that they deserve to be healthy and happy!

If you are feeling guilty, I would suggest that you have put yourself through enough. Why prolong it? If you were to feel guilty for an extra year or two, you wouldn't help things.

Throw out the guilt. Not that it's always easy to throw it out. Maintaining a healthy mind takes a lot of effort as does maintaining a healthy body. It is worth the effort.

IN A NUTSHELL

Blaming and feeling guilty are equally dangerous and destructive. While we blame God, blame others and blame ourselves, we are avoiding the real issue which is to do something about the problem. It is always OUR CHOICE whether we get on with our life and live in the now, or whether we chain ourselves to grudges and upsets of the past.

HAPPINESS

"Most people are about as happy as they make up their mind to be." So said Abraham Lincoln. It is not what happens to us in life that determines our happiness so much as the way we react to what happens.

Fred might, on just having lost his job, decide that he now has the opportunity to have a new work experience, to explore new possibilities and to exercise his independence in the workplace. His brother Bill might, under the same circumstances, decide to jump off a twenty storey building and end it all. Given the same situation, one man rejoices while the other man commits suicide! One man sees disaster and the other man sees opportunity.

I may have simplified things a little here but the fact remains that we decide how we react in life. (And even if we lose control, that is a decision that we make. We perhaps decide, "Things are getting a little too difficult for me. I think I will lose my mind for a while!")

Being happy is not always easy, though. It can be one of the greatest challenges that we face and can sometimes take all the determination, persistence and self-discipline that we can muster. Maturity means taking responsibility for our own happiness and choosing to concentrate on what we have got rather than on what we haven't.

We are necessarily in control of our own happiness as we decide the thoughts we think. No-one else puts thoughts in our mind. To be happy, we need to concentrate on happy thoughts. How often, though, do we do the opposite? How often do we ignore the compliments that are paid to us yet dwell on unkind words for weeks afterwards? If you allow a bad experience or nasty remark to occupy your mind, you will suffer the consequences. Remember, you are in control of your own mind.

Most people remember compliments for a few minutes and insults for years. They become garbage collectors, carrying around trash that was thrown at them twenty years ago. Mary may be heard to say, "I still remember how he said that I was fat and stupid back in 1963!" Any compliments Mary received even yesterday will probably have been forgotten but she is still carting around the 1963 trash.

"Be happy or else!"

I remember, age twenty five, waking up one day and deciding that I had had enough of being miserable. I thought to myself, "If you are going to be a really happy person someday, why don't you start now?" That day I decided to be a whole lot happier than I had ever been before. I was stunned. It actually worked!

I then began to ask other happy people how they came to be so happy. Invariably, their answer reflected my experience exactly. They would say, "I had had enough misery, heartache, loneliness and I DECIDED to change things."

IN A NUTSHELL

Being happy can be hard work sometimes. It is like maintaining a nice home — you've got to hang on to your treasures and throw out the garbage. Being happy requires looking for good things. One person sees the beautiful view and the other sees the dirty window. You choose what you see and you choose what you think.

Kazantzakis said, "You have your brush and colors. You paint paradise, then in you go."

PERFECTION AND HAPPINESS.

If we're unhappy, it's because life is not as we want it. Life is not matching our expectations of how it "ought" to be and so we're unhappy.

So we say, "I'll be happy when . . ." Well, life is NOT perfect. Life is about being exhilarated, frustrated, sometimes achieving and sometimes missing out. So long as we say "I'll be happy when . . .", we're deluding ourselves.

Happiness is a decision. Many people live life as if someday they'll arrive at "happiness" like one arrives at a bus stop. They figure that someday eveything will fall into place, they will take a deep breath and say,

"Here I am at last . . . happy!" Hence their life story is one of "I'll be happy when . . ."

Each one of us has a decision to make. Are we prepared to daily remind ourselves that we have only limited time to make the most of what we've got, or will we while away the present, hoping for a better future?

The following piece was written by an eighty-five-year old man who learned that he was dying. It is particularly relevant.

"If I had my life to live over again, I'd try to make more mistakes next time. I wouldn't be so perfect. I would relax more. I'd limber up. I'd be sillier than I've been on this trip. In fact, I know very few things that I would take so seriously. I'd be crazier. I'd be less hygienic.

"I'd take more chances, I'd take more trips, I'd climb more mountains, I'd swim more rivers, I'd go more places I've never been to. I'd eat more ice cream and fewer beans.

"I'd have more actual troubles and fewer imaginary ones!

"You see, I was one of those people who lived prophylactically and sensibly and sanely hour after hour and day after day. Oh, I've had my moments, and if I had it to do over again, I'd have more of those moments — moment by moment by moment.

"I've been one of those people who never went anywhere without a thermometer, a hot water bottle, a gargle, a raincoat and a parachute. If I had it to do all over again, I'd travel lighter next time.

"If I had it to do all over again, I'd start barefoot earlier in the spring and stay way later in the fall. I'd ride more merry-go-rounds, I'd watch more sunrises, and I'd play with more children, if I had my life to live over again.

"But you see, I don't."

Isn't this message a beautiful reminder? We only have so long on this planet. Let's make the most of it. The old man realized that, in order to be happier, in order to get more out of life, he didn't have to go and change the world. The world is already beautiful. He had to change himself.

The world is not "perfect". The degree of our unhappiness' is the distance between the way things are and the way they "ought" to be. If we cease to demand that things be perfect, the business of being happy becomes easier. We then choose to have preferences for the way things might be, and decide that if our preferences are not met, we will be happy anyway.

As the Indian guru once told a pupil who was in desperate search of contentment, "I will give you the secret. If you want to be happy, BE HAPPY!"

DEALING WITH DEPRESSION

Everyone of us goes through times when life seems extremely difficult — we are left alone, we can't pay the bills, we have lost our job, we have lost a loved one. At these times we wonder how we will possibly make it through the next week. Somehow we usually do!

It is possible to lose our perspective, and to paint the picture gloomier than it really is. We look toward a future which seems to be a minefield of problems and wonder how any human being could cope with what we face.

A person embarking on a day's march would be foolish to carry enough provisions for a lifetime. Is it not strange, then, that many people carry around all their worries for the next twenty five years and wonder why life is so difficult? We were designed to live twenty four hours at a time. No more. It is pointless worrying about tomorrow's problems today.

Next time you find yourself despairing, ask yourself these questions —

Have I got enough air to breathe? Have I enough food for today?

(If the answer is "Yes", things are already looking up!).

We often overlook the fact that our most important needs are being met. I like the story of the man who phoned Dr. Robert Schuller. The conversation went this way.

The man said, "It's over. I'm finished. All my money has gone. I've lost everything."

Dr. Schuller asked, "Can you still see?"

The man replied, "Yes, I can still see."

Schuller asked, "Can you still walk?"

The man said, "Yes, I can still walk."

Schuller said, "Obviously you can still hear or you would'nt have phoned me."

"Yes, I can still hear."

"Well," Schuller said, "I figure you have got about everything left. All you·have lost is your money!

Another question we can ask ourselves is, "What is the worst that could happen? And if it did, would I still be alive?" So often, we magnify things out of proportion. The worst that could happen is probably very inconvenient, but not the end of the world.

The next question to ask yourself is, "Am I taking myself too seriously?" Have you ever noticed that you can lose a week's sleep over something that your friends would never give a second thought? This is

often because we take ourselves too seriously. We figure the whole world is watching. It is not. And so what if it is? No doubt you are living your life the best way you know how.

Next question, "What am I learning from this situation?" With hindsight, looking through a "retrospectoscope", we can generally learn from our difficult times. The hard bit is being balanced and aware enough to learn while we are suffering — or why we are suffering. The happiest people tend to be able to always see their hard times as a valuable learning experience. They keep their chins up, they keep a smile on their faces, they know things will improve and that they will emerge from their trials better people. This is easier said than done!

Another question: If things really seem serious, will I be OK for the next five minutes? Once you have made it through those five minutes, just aim at getting through the next five. Bite off one small chunk at a time. It saves a lot of indigestion. Also, keep yourself busy. Give yourself a five minute job into which you can put your total energy. We always feel so much better when we are busy.

What else can I do?

Probably the greatest way to feel better about yourself is to do something for somebody else. Excessive worry and self-pity grow out of self-preoccupation. The moment you start to make other people happy, whether you are sending them flowers or digging their garden or giving them your time, you feel better! It is automatic. It is simple. And wonderful.

IN A NUTSHELL

Disasters aren't so disastrous if we tackle them a piece at a time. Also, the sooner we recognize what we stand to gain from the experience, the easier it is to deal with.

HUMOR

In Norman Cousins' book "Anatomy of an Illness", he tells how he recovered from a crippling disease to resume a healthy, normal life. His main medicine — laughter in large doses. Cousins believed that his serious approach to life had precipitated his illness and figured he could reverse the condition through laughter. He watched Marx Brothers movies and Candid Camera tapes until both the symptoms and the pain disappeared. He demonstrated what people have said for years, "Laughter is the best medicine."

When you laugh, all kinds of wonderful things happen to benefit your body and mind. Endorphins are released in your brain which give you a "natural high" and your respiratory system gets the kind of work-out that it may get from jogging.

Laughter relieves pain. You can only laugh when you are relaxed and the more relaxed you are the less pain you feel; so funny books and movies are ideal pain relievers. In fact, you can't get ulcers and laugh at the same time — you have to choose one or the other. The same goes for other illnesses. We often get sick by taking ourselves and life too seriously. What we need to do is laugh to help us stay healthy.

Let us assume that you are broke and you have just smashed your car, you are going through a divorce and the roof is leaking. If all that is going on, why make things worse by being unhappy as well?

The art of being happy involves being able to laugh at difficulties as soon as possible after they happen. One person, involved in the above situation, would resist laughing for two years. Another may decide that after two weeks it is time to stop crying and start laughing. Therefore, the first person gets to stay miserable for fifty times longer than the other one. AND HE CHOSE TO.

We all suffer misfortunes. HAPPY PEOPLE CHOOSE TO AVOID WAITING TOO LONG TO SEE THE FUNNY SIDE OF THEIR DISAPPOINTMENTS.

Periodically, let us remind ourselves that we are human and that we will do stupid things. If you expect to be perfect you don't belong on this planet. Let's remember that our own troubles always seem much bigger to us than to anyone else. If no-one else is losing sleep, maybe we don't need to either.

Children can teach us a lot about laughing. Happy youngsters will laugh at almost anything, naturally and unashamedly. They seem intuitively to know what a good belly laugh keeps them healthy and balanced. They come equipped with an insatiable thirst for joy and fun. It is a shame that by the time many reach adulthood this attitude has been replaced by one which says: "Life is all serious." Grown ups spend their time telling children when not to giggle and when not to laugh — "Don't laugh in class, don't giggle at the dinner table" — until much of their natural spontaneity is gone.

One of our major responsibilities toward others is to enjoy ourselves! When we are having fun, we feel better, we work better and people want to be around us.

IN A NUTSHELL

Life is not THAT serious. Let's take humor more seriously.

YOUR MIND

*Thoughts are invisible clouds that go out
and gather up results for us.
They determine what we reap.*

WE GRAVITATE IN THE DIRECTION OF OUR DOMINANT THOUGHTS

Let's spend some time examining how what is on your mind affects what is in your life. Perhaps one of the most important principles you will ever understand about your mind is that you will always gravitate toward what you think about most.

I met a woman recently who told me, "When I was young I said I would never marry a man called "Smith", I would never marry a man younger than myself and I would never wash dishes for a living. I have done all three!"

How often have you heard that kind of story? How often have you found yourself in precisely the situation that you said you didn't want? You said to yourself, "If there is one thing I don't want to happen . . . If there is one question I don't want to be asked . . . If there is one stupid mistake that I don't want to repeat . . . and guess what you got?"

"Serve another double fault and I'll break your neck!"

The principle is, "Think about something and you move toward it." Even if you are thinking about something you don't want, you will move toward it. This is because your mind moves toward things, never away from them. If I say to you, "Don't think about a big pink elephant with big ears and purple spots and wearing shades", what will fill your mind? An elephant!

Do you ever say to yourself, "I must not forget that" and then go and forget it? Your mind cannot move away from forgetting. It can move toward remembering but only if your thinking is "I want to remember that".

This awareness of how our mind works gives us cause to consider what we are saying to ourselves and to others. When you say to your little nephew, "Don't fall out of that tree", you are actually helping him to fall out of it! If you say to yourself "I don't want to forget my book", you are already half way to forgetting it.

This is because your mind works on pictures. When you say to yourself, "I don't want to forget my book", you get a picture in your mind of forgetting. Although you say "I don't want that", your mind still works on that picture and the result . . . you forget your book. When you tell yourself "I want to remember my book", you will have a mental picture of yourself remembering, and you will be in a far better position to remember.

Your mind simply does not, cannot and will not work on the reverse of an idea. Therefore when the football coach screams out to his player, 'Don't miss it", he is asking for trouble! When you say to your children, "Don't break grandma's ten thousand dollar antique vase", you are inviting disaster!

Many frustrated parents could ease their situations by using language which paints pictures of the desired result in their children's minds. Then 'Don't scream!' becomes "Please be quiet" and "Don't spill spaghetti on your best shirt" becomes "Be careful when you eat". These differences may seem subtle but they are very, very important.

This principle can help explain why you can drive your old wreck for fifteen years and never scratch it . . . and the first day you have your shiny new set of wheels, you manage to remodel the whole front end! Driving around thinking, "I mustn't dent this car whatever I do!" is a dangerous thought. The thought must be, I'll drive safely.

The tennis player who wins the big tournaments is the player who is always thinking, "I want this point. This one is mine!" The fellow who misses out is the one who thinks, "I had better not blow this shot!"

Similarly, the person who says "I don't want to be sick" has an uphill battle to become well and those who fill their minds with thoughts like "I don't want to be lonely", "I don't want to be broke" and "I hope I don't mess this up" can continually find themselves in the very situation they didn't want.

IN A NUTSHELL

Positive thinking works because positive thinkers dwell on what they want. They then necessarily gravitate toward their goals. Always think about what you want.

YOUR SUBCONSCIOUS

You are probably at least vaguely aware of the workings of your subconscious mind yet might have trouble defining exactly what it is. Hundreds of books have been written on the power of your subconscious mind.

In brief, what your subconscious mind believes is what you get. Its effect and control is so all embracing that the acknowledged father of American psychology, William James, labelled its discovery as the most important find of the last hundred years.

Your mind is like an iceberg in that while you are more aware of your outer or conscious mind, the part with the greater impact is the hidden part. All of your conscious thoughts contribute to the building of your subconscious mind. When you learned to eat with a knife and fork, it took a lot of conscious thought and effort. Over time, your deftness with your cutlery became a part of your subconscious program such that now you would rarely miss your mouth! Your bodily functions, your attitudes and all of your learned skills are keyed into your subconscious mind.

If you ask eighty-word per minute typists to tell you where the keys are on a typewriter, they will be in big trouble! They can hit five keys per second with their eyes shut using their subconscious mind, but they can't consciously tell you the arrangement of the letters unless they put their hands on the table and pretend to type! Fascinating, isn't it?

Claude Bristol in his book "The Magic of Believing" stated, "Just as the conscious mind is the source of thought, so the subconscious is the source of power." Your subconscious mind contains your "programs" for walking, talking, solving problems when you are asleep, healing your body, saving your life in times of danger and much, much more.

It includes the sum total of all your conscious thoughts up until now and whatever you have deposited into your subconscious mind by way of your day to day thoughts is now producing the results in your life. Your subconscious programs are responsible for your successes and your failures. Furthermore, it does not matter whether what your subconscious believes to be true is actually true. You will reap results consistent with what your inner programs say should happen.

For example, if you consistently walk, talk and think "success", then you will inevitably develop a subconscious expectancy of success. You will attract, and you will demonstrate it.

If in your thoughts you often entertain sickness and you talk of your own sickness, your subconscious will accept sickness patterns and you'll be open to ill health. When you fall ill you may have had no recent conscious thoughts of sickness. You may argue that you didn't want to be sick, never thought of being sick and never expected it either. However, your subconscious will have made you vulnerable and you will remain so until you reprogram your inner mind.

The subconscious mind is miraculous in its ability to solve problems. You may have experienced going to bed needing to find a solution to a problem. Finally, you decided to stop worrying and go to sleep. Next morning you awoke to find that your subconscious had found your answer and presented it to your conscious mind.

Trying to fully understand the workings of the mind is not an easy task, especially when we realize that the human brain is the most complex piece of equipment known to man!

IN A NUTSHELL

Acknowledge that, daily, you create programs in your subconscious by your thoughts, so watch what you think! Use your mind as all successful and happy people have used theirs. Use it as the great composers, scholars, artists, inventors and sportspeople have used their minds. Implant your goals into your subconscious as if they have already been achieved. For example, if you want to be a confident person, continue to see yourself brimming with confidence in your creative imagination. See the goal already achieved and your inner mind will set about producing your ideal end result.

If you want to be wealthy, use the same principle — continue to picture the ideal end result. Tell yourself that you are already enjoying the success and prosperity you desire and your inner mind will go to work for you. The principle works consistently and infallibly. Some people spend their time demanding logical explanations and trying to figure out how it all works while their neighbors are using these laws of the mind to get healthy, wealthy and rich. *"If it gets results, use it."* Work it out later.

IMAGINATION

"Imagination is more important than knowledge."
Einstein

"Imagination rules the world."
Disraeli

It has been estimated that we do about seventy percent of our learning in the first six years of our life, such is our ability in those early years to absorb new things. This is also the time when our imagination is most fertile.

The latter point explains the former. We need a good imagination in order to learn quickly and easily. Therefore we need to maintain a healthy respect for a creative imagination, and in fact to stimulate and develop it, throughout adulthood.

Sometimes a parent might be heard to say, "I'm worried about little Johnny; he has this incredible imagination!" Other parents seem to believe that the value of a child's imagination is in entertaining adults.

The simple truth is that the imagination is the key to all learning and all problem-solving, and hence the Edisons and the Einsteins of this world have all had excellent imaginations. For example, Albert Einstein arrived at his scientific conclusions about time and space by mentally projecting himself out among the planets where he would ride around on moonbeams. His ability to be childlike helped him to become a giant among intellectuals.

A good imagination is also important for a good memory. This is one reason why older people often report having bad memories — they have let their imagination deteriorate such that their mind will no longer create pictures which will "stick" in their mind. Whenever we record information in our memory banks, we use our imagination and our powers of visualization to create a picture. The effectiveness with which we create our picture determines how easily we recall the information.

In addition, a good imagination is essential in order to be able to relax your body and mind. For example, if you can totally involve yourself in an imaginary scene from nature, say the beach, then you will have the ability to relax at will. What a valuable asset! On the other hand, someone whose imagination is not so developed will have more trouble relaxing.

IN A NUTSHELL

Exercise your imagination as you do your body. The more you develop it, the easier it will be to solve problems and remember facts.

IMAGINATION AND DREAMERS

"The greatest achievement was at first and for a time a dream. The oak sleeps in the acorn; the bird waits in the egg; and in the highest vision of the soul a waking angel stirs. Dreams are the seedlings of realities."

James Allen.

We must cherish our imagination; our ability to dream; for the highest achievers since history began, have been the dreamers who, combined their perspiration and their aspiration to make their own unique contribution.

Leonardo Da Vinci, age twelve and illegitimate, vowed, "I shall become one of the greatest artists the world has ever known and one day I shall live with kings and walk with princes."

While a young boy, Napoleon spent long hours conquering Europe in his mind, dreaming of how he would lead and manage his troops. The rest is history.

The Wright brothers turned their dreams into airplanes, Henry Ford turned his dream of an affordable car for everybody into assembly line manufacturing.

Even as a child, Neil Armstrong dreamed of making his mark in the field of aviation. In July 1969, he became the first man to walk on the moon.

Everything starts as a dream. Stand by your dream. As the song says, "If you never have a dream, you'll never have a dream come true."

MENTAL REHEARSAL

Let's now have a look at how you can use your imagination to improve your performance at anything you do.

Some years ago, "Reader's Digest" published the results of an experiment conducted in a high school where students of roughly equal ability were divided into three groups to test their skills at throwing a basketball through a hoop. The first group practiced throwing free throws for one hour, every day for a month. The second group, the control group of the experiment, did no practice. Group number three practiced their free throws in their mind for an hour a day.

The group that physically practiced improved their average by two percent. The group that did no practice deteriorated by two percent. Group three, who only did mental practice, improved by three and one half percent!

This demonstrates what many people seem to know already — practicing in our imagination gets outstanding results. Do you ever mentally play a golf shot, rehearse an interview or mentally reverse into a car park before you actually do it? That is mental rehearsal and many of us do it without thinking in our daily lives. It is a childlike and imaginative process and its value is enormous.

Whenever you carry out an action, for example, hitting a golf ball, your body is responding to "programs" on your brain cells which, like a computer program, say "do this and do that". If you have a good program, you will hit good shots. If you have an "I can't do it program", then you'll do a lot of walking in long grass! Obviously as you practice out on the course, you gradually refine your automatic programs such that you hit better and better shots.

Now many people would believe that the only way to improve a skill, in this instance golfing, is to physically practice. Not so! Certainly you can repattern your brain cells through physically playing the game, but it is not the best way. The fastest way to improve at anything is to combine regular physical with regular mental practice.

Recent scientific discoveries prove that when you imagine yourself performing a task, you alter your mental programs as you do when you actually perform it. Your brain undergoes electro-chemical changes within its cells which produce new behavior. To take this a step further, it is fair to assume that we want these patterns on our brain cells to be as near to perfect as possible and the only place that you can perform perfectly is in your mind. So we see that for best results, we need mental as well as physical practice. You can improve your golf game, your public speaking, your confidence, your driving skills and any other abilities you choose, by sitting in an armchair and mentally rehearsing.

Controlled experiments have repeatedly proven this principle. In his classic book, "Psycho-Cybernetics", Dr. Maxwell Maltz quotes examples of darts players and basketball players who have significantly improve their performance with these techniques. Olympic athletes and professional sportspeople intuitively visualize, and so it is common to see them in the field with their eyes closed, practicing their sport. They are busy implanting patterns of brilliant performance into their subconscious minds which will ensure an improved game. I don't wish to negate the value of actual work and practice; I wish to stress the fact that visualizing perfect end results helps us to realize our potential much sooner and with less effort.

IN A NUTSHELL

The great value of mental rehearsal is that you can create patterns on your brain cells for perfect performance. In your imagination you need make no mistakes. From this we also learn that if we constantly imagine the results that we don't want, we will get those results! Many people live their whole lives that way — thinking about what they fear most and wondering why it always happens to them! I'll talk more about this later.

From now on, make a habit of refining your abilities through your imagination. Whether you will be teaching a class, walking into a room of strange people, making a difficult phone call or riding a windsurfer for the first time; spend some time doing it perfectly in your mind beforehand. The world's most successful people are doing it already — join them.

WE GET WHAT WE EXPECT

We tend to attract what we expect in life. The tennis player says, "I must wear my rabbit's foot or I won't win." While he tells himself that, he is right. But it is not the furry little paw that has all the power; it is the mind of the player. So much for black cats and Friday the thirteenths and walking under ladders.

If Mary says, "People only come to visit me when my house is in a mess," she will find that pattern repeating. If husband Fred says that he gets a cold every year, you can bet he will. If Fred says, "Whenever I get some spare cash together, I always get an unexpected expense that wipes me out," Fred will keep getting wiped out.

Doctors find that their patients tend to heal in accordance with their expectations, rather than healing as the prognosis would suggest. Dr. Carl Simonton, in his work with cancer sufferers in the U.S.A., has made particular note of how his patients' recovery repeatedly reflect their expectations of recovery.

"Four thirty pm! I should be getting my migraine any minute!"

One person says, "People always ignore me, treat me badly, rip me off," and finds that that is what life deals him. Another person says, "People always treat me well," and he is treated well.

IN A NUTSHELL

What does all this tell us? It tells us that you are in control. You decide what you think. You decide what you put in your mind and so determine what you get back.

Look for people who are really happy. They are hard to find! Look for people who are leading rotten lives and expect life to be wonderful. They are equally hard to find. We get from life largely what we expect.

THE LAW OF ATTRACTION

Have you ever been thinking of somebody whom you had not seen in months, and had them arrive on your doorstep that very morning? Have you ever written to a friend after years of no communication and had your letters cross? Have you ever been singing an old song in your head and found it playing on the radio when you turned it on?

Have you ever decided to get your hands on a particular book or record, and found yourself stumbling across it just hours later? Have you found yourself with the job or the house that you had imagined having years before, and wondered whether there was something more than your own conscious effort to thank for the achievement of your goal?

Such occurrences are grouped by many people under the label of coincidence, but there is something greater at work here. Your mind is a magnet and you attract what you think about. The same principles of magnetism and attraction which we observe at work in the "physical" world, are at work on the invisible plane.

When my attention was first drawn to this, I thought, "What a lot of garbage! How could my mind possibly attract, produce or manifest anything?" However, I thought the matter was worthy of further investigation on the off-chance that some other screwballs might subscribe

to the same theory. Just in case it was actually true that our mind does attract things, I didn't want to be the pitiful individual who spent a whole life in struggle due to his own ignorance!

I went out and bought myself some books on the mind; some scientific, some metaphysical, some spiritual, some about getting rich. To my surprise, each of the volumes I bought came to similar conclusions regarding the magnetic nature of the human mind. Coincidence, I thought! I bought some more books ... and then some more. I read about two hundred. They were written by various authors from all over the world in different times and by people of different religious and philosophical persuasions. They all said basically the same thing — "You attract what you hold in your mind. Your mind is a magnet." I was starting to think there might be something in this.

I started to use my mind as was recommended in the books and that is when I really became convinced! I now teach seminars on the effective use of the mind where my students learn how to get on the good side of the way things work.

LISTEN TO THOSE WHOSE LIVES ARE WORKING

One of the first things I found out about these laws of attraction and the miracle of the mind is that all the successful people know about these principles already! I would tell them about one of my latest discoveries to which they would invariably reply, "I have been using this stuff for years."

I also found that the most miserable people I came across would generally dispute that any such principles can work in our favor. I choose to take the advice of those who are happy with their lives rather than those who gripe!

We could fill volumes with what has been said by various authors on the creative power of the mind, but in the interests of brevity I will quote from just a few.

In his classic bestselling book, "Think and Grow Rich", Napoleon Hill wrote, ". . . our brains become magnetized with the dominating thoughts which we hold in our minds and, by means with which no man is familiar, these "magnets" attract to us the forces, the people, the circumstances of life which harmonize with the nature of our dominating thoughts."

James Allen wrote in "As a Man Thinketh", ". . . a man sooner or later discovers that he is the master-gardener of his soul, the director of his life. He also reveals, within himself, the laws of thought, and understands, with ever increasing accuracy, how the thought-forces and mind elements operate in the shaping of his character, circumstances and destiny." He added, "That circumstances grow out of thought every man knows who has for any length of time practiced self control . . "

In "The Magic of Believing", Claude Bristol again speaks of the mind's power to attract. "Our fear thoughts are just as creative or just as magnetic in attracting troubles to us as the constructive and positive thoughts in attracting positive results. So no matter what the character of the thought it does create after its own kind. When this sinks into a man's consciousness, he gets some inkling of the awe-inspiring power which is his to use." He later says, "What may appear as coincidences are not coincidences at all but simply the working out of the pattern which you started with your own weaving."

In offering some explanations of the mind's power to attract, Bristol makes the point that radio waves pass easily through wood, brick, steel and other so-called solid objects and suggests that we might see thought vibration in a similar light. He asks the question, "If thought waves, or whatever they are, can be tuned to even higher oscillations, why can't they affect the molecules of solid objects?"

I quote Shakti Gawain, author of "Creative Visualisation" on the same theme. She says, "Thought and feelings have their own magnetic energy which attracts energy of a similar nature ... This is the principle that whatever you put out into the universe will be reflected back to you. What this means from a practical standpoint is that we always attract into our lives whatever we think about most, believe in most strongly, expect on the deepest levels, and/or imagine most vividly."

Richard Bach wrote, "We magnetize into our lives whatever we hold in our thoughts."

A thought is not a "nothing", but a "something". In order for you to think it, it must exist. It must be a thing! And as it is a "thing" with an energy of its own, a thought must necessarily be bound by laws and principles like everything else on this planet.

Perhaps seen in this light it is easier to acknowledge that the law of attraction is as real and as powerful as gravity and electricity.

The list could go on and on. My object in writing this book is to provide some clarity for you, the reader, as to how your mind creates the results you reap. I would not wish that you blindly accept these concepts without trial. Also, I wish to stress strongly here as I do elsewhere in the book, that *the harnessing of your thought power is not a substitute for action. Rather, the proper use of your mind will enable you to achieve your goals far more quickly and easily than you otherwise would.*

IN A NUTSHELL

Your mind is a magnet. Continue to dwell on what you want and you will achieve it.

Think of your thoughts as invisible clouds which go out and gather up results for you. By disciplining your thoughts, you determine what you reap.

WE ATTRACT WHAT WE FEAR

s the things that we most love and most fear will tend to occupy our thoughts much of the time, so will we tend to attract those very things. Have you ever totally ruined a

new suit of clothes the very first time you wore them? Just as you were thinking to yourself, "I don't want to dirty this lovely new shirt of mine", your ball point pen was leaking blue ink into your top pocket.

How often does it happen that somebody says, "I drove a beaten up old wreck for seven years and never even scratched it. As soon as I got my lovely new set of wheels, people started driving into the back of me, side-swiping me and running me off the road".

I spoke earlier of the woman who has had five accidents in seven years. At last she has realized that she has dwelt so much on her fears that she has attracted what she did not want.

Even if we say to our mind, "I don't want "A" to happen, we will gravitate toward "A". Our mind cannot move away from anything, only toward something.

This explains why as a child you could sneak into an empty kitchen, arm yourself with a month's supply of cookies, turn to effect your silent and stealthy exit and ... CAUGHT! Suddenly, out of nowhere, Father had appeared. Your major thought was, "I'll just grab these cookies and I hope I don't get caught or I'm dead." You got caught!

You may also have had the experience of being on a date and thinking, "Wouldn't it be embarrassing if my ex-lover showed up". Needless to say, your greatest fear was realized.

Have you ever had a party or special event coming up and entertained the thought, "I hope I don't get sick and miss out on this" You got sick and missed out, didn't you? Fascinating how our minds work, isn't it?

A magazine recently published an article about a New Yorker by the name of Pete Torres who, at the time of publication of the story, had been mugged fifteen times since 1968. This we believe may be some dubious kind of record. While Pete proclaims that he is doing nothing to precipitate these attacks, he is in fact helping to bring the misery upon himself. His secret passion is watching horror movies. He spends all his spare time loading up on stabbings and muggings and robberies. He fills his mind with horror stories, obviously enjoys being "scared", and wonders why life on the streets of New York is one long horror story.

We can see the same principles working with poverty and ill health. If we talk about, read about and think about "nasties", we will subconsciously if not consciously gravitate toward them. Successful people move toward success. Failures try to run away from failures. If there is one mental principle which can transform losers into achievers, it is the "concentrate on what you want" principle.

It is laughable to go into the corner store and say to the assistant, "I don't want milk. I don't want bread. I don't want cheese," and expect to return home satisfied. Yet most people stagger through life bemoaning what they don't have and talking about what they don't want. It is a hopeless situation. We must focus on what we want.

Expanding on this theme, we discover the "fear of loss" principle. When we fear losing something, we place ourselves in a position to lose it. This applies to husbands, girlfriends, wallets, tennis matches and stereo systems.

From time to time we read about people in the newspapers who continually have their homes burgled. Regardless of the locks, detection systems, chains, bolts and barking German Shepherds, it always seems to be open house for cat burglars.

These laws work equally powerfully in relationships. When we fear losing somebody's love or affection, we are immediately in jeopardy of losing it. The message must surely be, "Concentrate on and enjoy what you have. Don't dwell on losing what you have."

Focus on what you want. Dwelling on your fears will bring them upon you. The principle of attracting what we fear is actually quite wonderful. It means that we are challenged to confront fear and hence to improve ourselves. How else would we grow if the things we feared ran away from us? How else would we develop if we never faced the things we feared?

With regard to fearing loss, the laws of the universe prod us to stand on our own two feet. If we get the idea that the loss of something will wreck our lives, and dwell on that thought, then the universe may decide to prove to us that we can live without it!

If you decide that it is impossible for you to live without your Porsche 911, then the universe may well help you to experience life without it. When your attitude is, "I enjoy my car and I can be just as happy without it," you will get to hang on to it for as long as you want. Circumstances assist us in learning about and strengthening ourselves.

We need to enjoy what we have right now and live right now. Fearing loss is not living in the now. Fearing loss is living in the future.

WHEN WE CONFRONT FEARS THEY DISAPPEAR.

Another fascinating principle is that often, when we finally develop the courage to meet a problem head on, the problem disappears and we don't have to face it.

As soon as we develop the courage to make the difficult phone call, confront our employee or make the sacrifice, very often it becomes unnecessary. We agonize for weeks over breaking the news to our secretary that she'll need to find alternative employment and when we finally hit her with the news, she tells us that she can't wait to leave! Of course, this turn of events doesn't always occur and sometimes we have to bite the bullet!

Also, we often find that once we decide to face a fear, fear evaporates. No doubt you have had the experience of performing a task that you thought would be difficult or particularly embarrassing. When you jumped in and did it it wasn't half as bad as you anticipated. This particularly applies to telling the truth and owning up to mistakes and misdeeds. How often have you found that thinking about it was so much more painful than doing it?

THE POWER OF WORDS

"Thou shalt decree a thing and it shall be established unto thee."
Job 22. 28

What you say is what you get. As our thoughts affect our circumstances, so do the words we say. Our words build our attitude and they determine what we will attract and experience.

When we get serious about being happy, we stand guard over our mouth. We decide to speak positively about ourselves and avoid running ourselves down. This is not to pretend that we are perfect, but is a part of realizing that you can't feel good about yourself by grizzling about yourself, your job, your friends and family and everyone else about you.

A fellow came to me recently and said, "I'm tired of being miserable and depressed. I'm tired of being a burden to my family. I want to be happy! How do I do it?"

I said, "The first thing you can do is to open your mouth only when you have something positive and constructive to say. You will appreciate the change and so will your family!"

I saw him a week later and he was still griping. He said to me, "I want to be happy and I'm not. How can I do it? I said, "I gave you my best advice last week!"

He said, "I'm still not happy." I replied, "I know. That is because you are not serious enough about it yet! When you are really serious, you will be happy."

I still don't know whether he has gotten the message yet. He needs to recognize that he is the only person running his mouth. At some stage he will need to take responsibility for his own thoughts. He will need to get serious about what thoughts he has in his head.

It is very simple. When anybody has really, really had enough of being miserable, they change their attitude. They change the way they talk. It takes discipline, it takes effort, but it is still very simple. To discipline what we allow ourselves to think and say requires us to be different from the crowd. Excellence always does.

Some people adopt the attitude, "I'll do anything to be happier so long as I don't have to change anything about myself." Unfortunately, that usually isn't a big enough commitment to improvement!

Too often, the issue of mental health is made too complex. Patients go

to the doctor or the psychiatrist and get their condition labelled. Now they have something to blame — their "condition". Now there is a monster, almost with a life of its own — their "sickness."

The patient may have experienced a lot of trauma and pain and frustration up until now. The person no doubt deserves our love and support and empathy. However, the kindest thing that anyone can do for them is to help them to recognize their own responsibility. The issue remains, what is this person going to do starting tomorrow to become a happy person?

Words affect our personal power.

The words that we use are always filtering into our subconscious mind and becoming a part of our character and our make-up. They tell others exactly how serious and how committed we are to getting results.

There are some words which will generally undermine our progress. Every time we use the word "try", we indicate that we are not in control. If you are going to "try" and do a good job, "try" and arrive on time, "try" and be happy, you are suggesting that you may do it and you may not. Substituting a word like "will" for "try" is challenging and confronting, and will get us much better results. This may seem like detail, yet it is important in shaping the way we and others see us.

Using the words "I can't" can also undermine your personal power. Saying "won't" instead of "can't" will usually be closer to the truth. For example, "I won't see you tomorrow" indicates that you are in control and you have made the decision. "I won't learn to swim" means you are not prepared to put in the effort. You can if you really, really want to!

Words affect our memory.

Lots of people put great effort into telling others what a rotten memory they have. And what is their memory like? Rotten! We get what we expect, and our words affect our performance.

With regard to our memory, researchers now tell us that we never really forget anything. The information is all in our head. The problem is the recall. This explains why you can "forget" somebody's name and remember it next day. The name did not vacate your head and pop back into it twenty four hours later. It was there all the time but you could not "recall" it initially.

Our words affect our subconscious and our memory is closely linked with our subconscious. If you consistently give your subconscious a program that says "I remember things", then you will find that your recall will dramatically improve. You will subconsciously expect to remember the names and the numbers and you will do so more and more.

AFFIRMATIONS

An affirmation is a positive thought that you repeat to yourself. Using affirmations allows you to select quality thoughts and implant them into your subconscious so that you can feel better and perform better.

Let's assume that you are out driving on the highway and you have a splitting headache. Here is your opportunity to combine the power of words with the power of thought. You begin to repeat to yourself, "My head feels wonderful!" or "My head is relaxed and at ease."

As you begin to tell yourself this, no doubt a little voice in the background will be saying, "You lying hound. You feel terrible!"

However, if you continue with the positive affirmations, the thought that you are feeling well will take root in your subconscious. You will indeed start to feel better and a half an hour later, chances are the thought will cross your mind, "I had a headache, a while back. It has gone now. Was that the affirmations, or is this just coincidence?"

You can use affirmations to get results in a variety of areas.
For example, on the tennis court:
"I will play a good game."
In your relationships:
"People always treat me with love and respect. I treat all people with love and respect."

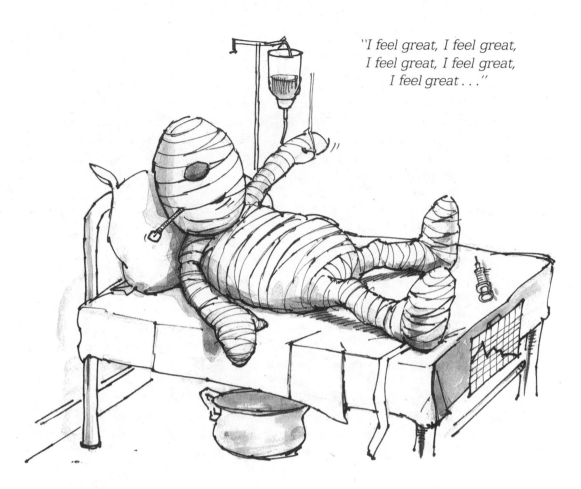

*"I feel great, I feel great,
I feel great, I feel great,
I feel great . . ."*

For your mental attitude:

"Every day in every way I am getting better and better and better."
For your prosperity:

"I feel healthy, I feel good and I feel prosperous.

The possibilities are endless. Affirmations will not mean that you never need to put in any effort. They will mean that you have a short cut to conditioning your mind for whatever you want. If you choose to make them a regular part of your life, you will find that they are a very simple and powerful tool. In fact they are almost too simple.

They are not complicated or sophisticated, and if you are a sophisticated person you may think, "I am not going to use that third grade stuff!" with the result that in a year's time you are still sophisticated, you still have headaches and you are still not using your mind to its maximum. Again, we each have a choice.

There are some rules to keep in mind when using affirmations. Firstly, as we discussed earlier, your mind will always move toward what you think about. Therefore if you design an affirmation like, "I won't argue with my husband," or "I am not sick," you won't be thrilled with the results! Your mind will keep moving you towards what you say you don't want. If you think about it, you may know of people who spend all their time talking about what they don't want, and wondering why they always get it.

I recall some of my school teachers used to have my classmates and me writing lines like, "I won't talk in class", and "I won't be late," and "I won't throw things at the teacher." Little did they realize that, structured in that negative vein, they were actually promoting misbehavior. As I reflect on what used to happen in my classes, I would have to concede that they did this very effectively!

The second principle to keep in mind with affirmations is that affirmations are much more effective when you say them out loud or write them down. If you just think your affirmations, your mind will tend to wander to other things like, "What's for lunch?" and "Where are the kids?" Saying or writing them keeps your mind on track. You also involve more of your physical senses when you speak or write, and hence the effect is more powerful.

The third thing to bear in mind with affirmations is that repetition is important. If you are wanting to restructure a belief system that you have had for twenty years, it will require some persistence. Don't expect to turn the course of your life around with six "I am really happy's!"

IN A NUTSHELL

Our words affect how we think and how we feel. What we think affects what we say and how we feel. How we feel influences what we say and how we think. Hence we have a vicious triangle.

If we are feeling low, it is easier to change what we say than change what we think and feel — it is easiest to give ourselves a fresh start by controlling what we say. Very shortly, what we are saying will start to have a positive effect on our thoughts and feelings. We will then have broken the vicious triangle and will be on our way to feeling better about things.

AN ATTITUDE OF GRATITUDE

I remember as a child being reminded that I should be grateful for all the good things I had in my life. My mother told us to say grace, say our prayers and to be thankful for loving parents, plenty of food, a warm bed, brothers and sisters, our good health and all the other things that I took for granted.

I even recall times when I was sent to my bedroom with a pencil and paper to make a list of all the things that I was grateful for! (This would invariably follow an outburst from me where I had expounded on how everything in the world was rotten and how I never got anything that I wanted). The list never got written and I could see absolutely no value in the exercise. If God happened to exist, I saw no point in giving Him the attention that I could be giving my tennis game.

Some years later I was able to place the "attitude of gratitude" into a whole different perspective. As I discovered more of how our minds work, and began to see that we have in our lives what we think about, and that we tend to get what we subconsciously expect, it registered that in order to continue to enjoy good fortune, I needed to feel fortunate.

It is imperative that we are thankful for what we have, not only from a spiritual point of view, but also from a scientific point of view. The great spiritual teachers; Jesus, Buddha, Mohammed and others, have taught that we should count our blessings. The wisdom behind this is that our mind is a magnet and we gravitate toward what we think about most.

If Fred continues to grizzle that nothing ever works for him, that there is never enough money, nobody loves him, he always gets the rotten jobs and life is tough, then he will necessarily attract more of the same. On the conscious level, he will overlook opportunity, refuse offers of assistance, and continue to propel himself into financial and emotional bankruptcy. On the subconscious level he will repel opportunity and attract one drama after another as he sees his world unfold precisely as he anticipated. Fred's picture of things is that he misses out and goes without and he will create a life for himself in accordance with his belief system.

My observation has been that the universe is essentially fairly forgiving, but that if a person consistently concentrates on what he doesn't have, he will get less and less of what he wants. I have also found that those people who have the most beautiful friendships are those people who value them very highly. Those who lead active and fulfilling lives are the people who are consistently rejoicing in what life gives them.

It appears that in many cases we are socially conditioned to look at the negative side of life. If there are ten things going right and one thing wrong, we tend to draw attention to what is wrong. When Junior gets eleven out of twenty in a maths test, we don't concentrate on the eleven he got right but on the nine that he missed. When we have a headache, we don't say "My chest, stomach, legs and arms feel great!" We say, "My head hurts!" We worry about the lipstick on our collar and don't rejoice in the fact that ninety nine percent of our shirt is clean! Too many people believe that being realistic and being rational is a matter of focusing on faults!

Somebody once commented, "If you are miserable about all the things you want but haven't got, think about all the things you don't want and haven't got!" There is a positive side to everything!

IN A NUTSHELL

An attitude of gratitude ensures that our attention is on what we want. As we see ourselves as living abundantly and richly, and recognize what we already have, we set up a flow of good things coming our way. More and more often, we find ourselves in the right place at the right time. It is an excellent system, really. What if the reverse were true, and the more we grizzled and moaned, and the less we did, the more we got?

CHAPTER 4

GOALS

Out on the limb is where the fruit is . . .

GOALS

"Life asks of every individual a contribution and it is up to that individual to discover what it should be."

Viktor Frankl

This chapter is about setting and reaching goals; why we should set them and some principles to keep in mind as we pursue them.

Frankl, in his classic book, "Man's Search for Meaning", wrote of life in a concentration camp during World War II. He calculated that only one person in twenty eight survived the horror of the camps and he made a personal study as to why one man would survive while many others perished.

He observed that the person who survived was not necessarily the fittest or the healthiest or the best-fed or the most intelligent. What he did find was that those who made it through had a reason to keep going. They had a GOAL. In Frankl's case, his burning desire was to see his wife's face again. Other survivors had different goals, but all had major goals nevertheless.

Goals are what keep us going. How often do we hear of someone retiring after forty years and dropping dead within a few short months? Once we lose our momentum, once we lose our direction, we are in trouble! Have you noticed that you have generally been happiest when in the middle of a project, and not at the end of it? Have you ever found that as soon as you finish a project, you look around for something else?

Let's recognize two major points here.

IT IS OUR NATURE TO HAVE GOALS. We can't live without them, or at least not for very long. Therefore, if you don't have yourself a list right now, you need one.

IT IS NOT SO IMPORTANT WHAT THE GOAL IS, SO LONG AS YOU HAVE ONE! Some people manage to continually postpone doing what they think they might like to do with their life. They are unsure as to whether the goal they have in mind is the perfect one for them, so they never do anything!

Take Bill Smith who is thinking about going back to school and getting a degree. He is just not quite sure whether it is the right thing for him. The trouble is, he has been making up his mind for the last thirty years and he is now fifty seven! He doesn't have much time left.

If Bill goes back to his studies and finds it is not for him, then that is wonderful. Now, at last he knows. You see, people often say, "What a tragedy it will be if I choose the wrong direction!" "What if I choose a goal and it turns out to be the wrong one, and it doesn't make me happy?" Actually, it is wonderful. They have now eliminated an additional possibility and they know more about what will make them happy and what will not.

Here we return to the issue where successful people see a wrong direction as a valuable learning experience while unsuccessful, unhappy people see a wrong direction as a failure.

THE LAW OF PRECESSION

Buckminster Fuller, recognized as one of this century's most creative minds, wrote of the "law of precession" as a part of the goal-setting process.

"Precession" is the principle which always ensures that we gain many things in addition to the actual goal itself. In fact, the most important thing is not the reaching of the goal but what we learn and how much we grow along the way.

Fred may say, "I spent six years at university just to get this bit of paper!" What he is failing to acknowledge is that he also met a lot of people, learned a lot about himself and had a lot of experiences that he otherwise would not have had. It is not the bit of paper that is important but the journey he took.

If you decide that you are going to walk across Europe or own a Ferrari sports car or start your own business, the important thing is not the walk or the car or the business, but what kind of person you need to become in order to achieve your end.

In pursuit of your goals, you may develop greater courage and determination, refine your powers of persuasion, learn about personal discipline, develop your stamina, learn to fly an airplane, achieve greater self-confidence, meet your life partner or learn to write a check!

What you GET in pursuit of your goals is of lesser importance. The real question is, "What will you BECOME?"

When setting out for a goal, it is worthwhile remembering the way things work on this planet. Nothing travels in straight lines. No goals are achieved without setbacks.

When the tide comes in, it comes in a bit and goes out a bit, but gradually it makes its way in. When a tree grows, it loses leaves from time to time, and each time it grows a few extra to compensate for the losses. The net result is that the tree gets bigger but it does not do without some loss and some struggle. The way things work on this planet is that setbacks are a part of the plan of things.

Unfortunately, some people have the idea that their own personal progress should defy all the laws of the universe. Therefore Mary starts on her lose weight program and finding that her progress is up and down, decides that losing weight for her is too hard or impossible, and spends the rest of her life as a fat girl. Fred starts a savings program and after one or two unforeseen expenses, concludes that it is impossible to save money and abandons all hope of ever achieving financial independence.

Successful people are not that brilliant or talented or unique. They simply have a grasp of the way things work and realize that their own progress will be in accordance with the principles that govern everything else around them.

They realize that we reach our goals by continually correcting. We get off-course, correct, and get back on course. Ships do it. Rockets and missiles do it. Correct. Correct. Correct.

ANOTHER REASON FOR HAVING GOALS

We have already discussed how we gravitate toward what we think about most. If you have some definite goals in mind, your thoughts will help to take you there as you will tend to be dwelling on your goals. If you have no goals, your thoughts will still take you toward what you think about most. Your mind will take your dominant thoughts and propel you in that direction, assuming that your dominant thoughts are your goals.

WRITE DOWN YOUR GOALS

I have observed that all motivational speakers that I have ever heard, have one thing in common. They all suggest, instruct, plead, insist that we write our goals down.

When you go shopping, you make a list. You do this so that you will come back from the store with what you wanted. A list keeps you on track. If you go out for some lunch, you don't want to arrive back saying to yourself, "What am I doing with this screwdriver? I went out for a hamburger!"

People make great long lists for parties. They list the napkins and the drinks and the cakes and the cookies to be sure that they have everything they want.

The strange thing is that although people realize that lists work, only about three percent ever use them for putting their life together. For their most important event, their life, most people stumble along blindly, never making a list of what they want, and all the time wondering why they never get it!

Making a list is not the only thing we need to do, but it gives us a method and a structure in achieving what we want out of life. Still, most people spend more time planning birthday parties than they do planning their lives; and then they wonder why they are not as happy as they could be.

Lists work! They work for shopping and they work for life.

IN A NUTSHELL

Goals are the vehicles whereby we can become someone more than we already are. We need goals, not for what they get for us but for what they do for us.

LIMITATIONS

"Whether you think you will succeed or not, you are right".
Henry Ford

The only thing that limits our achievements is the thought that we can't achieve. It is really not news to anybody that people who say they can, can, and people who say they can't, can't.

One man says, "I guess I will always be a battler." He stops learning, ignores opportunity, won't work late, won't save, won't try because "it is no use anyway". Lo and behold, his prophecy is proven correct. He never makes it.

Another man says, "I will succeed. I will do whatever it takes. I will work as long as I need to. I will learn as much as I can. I will be as different as I need to be. I can do it!" And the man does it!

It is worthwhile remembering that there are pay-offs in both approaches. The first fellow gets to avoid responsibility. He can always say, "It is all too difficult — you do it for me". He escapes having to exercise the personal discipline which would bring about his success. He may even get

some sympathy. Playing dumb and incapable can be very smart and very convenient.

The fruits enjoyed by the second fellow are more obvious. He reaches his goal. Let's recognize that there are advantages in both approaches.

IN A NUTSHELL

Whatever limitations we place upon ourselves are our responsibility. Throwing out the labels we hang on ourselves is the first step towards living the good life.

HANDICAPS

Whenever we doubt our own ability to achieve, it is worthwhile pondering the obstacles that others have overcome. To name a few, Demosthenes, the outstanding Greek orator suffered from a such a serious speech impediment that he could scarcely speak. He practiced talking with a mouth full of pebbles, figuring that when he had mastered that he would be able to speak in public. He became one of the great orators of all time.

Napoleon overcame his considerable handicap, his tiny stature, to lead his conquering armies across Europe.

Helen Keller refused to allow her blindness and her deafness to prevent her from spending her life helping those less fortunate than herself.

Abraham Lincoln failed in business age 31, lost a legislative race at 32, again failed in business at 34, had his sweetheart die when he was 35, had a nervous breakdown at 36, lost congressional races age 43, 46 and 48, lost a senatorial race at 55, failed in his efforts to become vice president of the U.S.A. age 56 and lost a further senatorial contest at 58.

At sixty years of age he was elected president of the U.S.A. and is now remembered as one of the great leaders in world history.

Anwar Sadat started his life as a peasant boy.

Menachim Begin was a street urchin in a Polish ghetto.

Winston Churchill was a poor student with a speech impediment. Not only did he win a Nobel Prize at twenty four, but he became one of the most inspiring speakers of recent times.

Thomas Edison was kicked out of school.

Atlas, the man who built a "perfect" body, was originally a ninety seven pound weakling.

Julio Iglesias was kicked out of his high school choir. That didn't stop him from becoming the biggest selling recording artist in the history of the world.

Alan Bond came to Australia a penniless immigrant signwriter at the age of fourteen. Not too many years later, as an international business tycoon, he mounted the America's Cup campaign which wrested the auld mug from the U.S.A. for the first time in 125 years.

The list goes on and on. The moral must surely be, "IT IS NOT WHERE YOU START THAT COUNTS, BUT WHERE YOU CHOOSE TO FINISH." Handicaps are a blessing if we choose to see them that way and use them as incentive to do better, and better.

PROBLEMS

"We are continually faced by great opportunities brilliantly disguised as insoluble problems.

The thought can occur to us from time to time, "Wouldn't it be great if we didn't have any problems?" We could just laze on the beach all day doing absolutely nothing. You could be like a shellfish. Shellfish don't worry that much about anything, as far as we can tell.

I suggest though, that after about eight years of lying on the sand contemplating your navel, you might be a little desperate for some challenge to present itself.

We are designed to solve problems and to find new ways of doing things. Problems are an inherent part of the universe and they prod us to learn, experience, to get off our backsides. Dogs are not great problem-solvers. If you are a dog, you get to take things easy. A pig has an even more relaxed approach to life. But who wants to be a pig?

The unique thing about being human is that you get to experience so much more. You can create something out of nothing. Pigs don't write music. Dogs don't build companies. Shellfish don't go to the movies. The package deal in being a human involves problems, and it also means we get to love, to laugh, to cry, to try, to get up and to fall down and get up again.

The positive thinker says that a problem is simply an opportunity to learn. This may sound like an old cliché but there is good sense in that philosophy, and babies and young children tend to live by it. Ten-month-old babies see everything as a challenge: the chance to make new noises, the opportunity to learn to pick things up, the challenge of eating, of throwing things, the fun of throwing what they are eating: life for them is a fascinating journey of discovery. Youngsters throw themselves at life with such beautiful reckless enthusiasm; racing bikes and running up ladders, leaping into surf and out of trees!

If you stop to think about it, some of the greatest challenges you ever faced were in your first few years, as you took on the problems of walking, talking, running, and so on. What is more, you managed all these things!

Somehow, active children can grow into scared adults of such timidity that the tiniest of tasks loom as insurmountable monsters. It is fortunate that many adults don't start out their lives with their "I'll never be able to do that" attitude, or they would still be helpless and lost, age forty six!

Is it not crazy that we expect more of children than we do of adults? We say to them in school, "Either you learn how to spell "cat" and "rat" and learn all those letters of the alphabet or you will stay in first grade". In other words, we give them the message that they had better perform or else. Unfortunately, many grown ups don't get the same message!

At some stage many adults get the notion that life should automatically reward them for no effort on their part. Shouldn't we adults demand similar progress from ourselves and ask, "What have I learned in the last twelve months? What can I do this year that I couldn't do last year?"

IN A NUTSHELL

Problems require us to stretch. As Horace said, "Adversity reveals genius, prosperity conceals it."

MISTAKES

There was a fellow lamenting the fact that God never spoke to him. "Why doesn't the Good Lord ever send me any messages like he seems to send other people?" he asked of his friend. "But the Lord does communicate with you", assured his buddy. "He communicates with you through your mistakes".

Mistakes are feedback on how we are doing. Winners make far more mistakes than losers. That is why they are winners. They are getting more feedback as they continue to try more possibilities. The only trouble with losers is that they regard a mistake as such a big event while failing to recognize the positive side to making mistakes.

We learn far more from our losses than we do from our victories. When we lose, we contemplate, we analyse, we regroup, we plan a new strategy. When we win, we simply celebrate, and learn very little! Another reason to welcome our errors!

The story of Thomas Edison is legendary, where a particular gentleman inquired of the inventor how it felt to have failed so many times in his efforts to produce an electric light bulb. Edison replied that he had not failed at all, but rather he had successfully found thousands of ways how not to make a light bulb! That kind of healthy atittude toward mistakes enabled Edison to make a contribution to the world which rivals that of almost anyone in history.

Werner von Braun was also aware that mistakes are an essential

ingredient in
the learning process.
During the Second World War
he was developing a rocket with
which the Germans hoped to bomb
London. His superiors called him before
them after some considerable time and
confronted him. He had made 65,121 mistakes thus far. They asked him,
"How many more mistakes until you get it right?"?

He replied that he thought another five thousand or so should do it!
He said, "It takes 65,000 errors before you are qualified to make a rocket.
Russia has made maybe 30,000 of them by now. America hasn't made
any." Throughout the latter half of the war, Germany pounded her
enemies with von Braun's ballistic missiles. No other country had such

weapons. Some years later, von Braun became a mastermind with America's space program which saw a man in the moon by 1969.

Columbus went looking for the quicker route to India and found America!

Laminated glass, where a slice of plastic is sandwiched between two sheets of glass, was first produced by accident. Its shatterproof qualities have since saved thousands of lives. Mistakes and accidents have their purpose.

The man who founded I.B.M., Thomas J. Watson, said "The way to succeed is to double your failure rate."

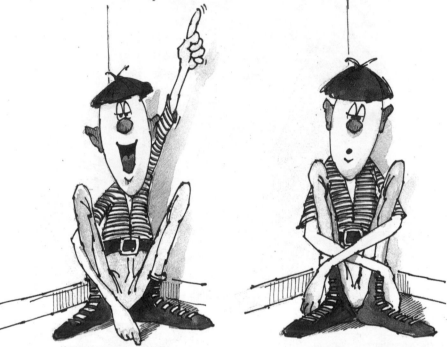

"I've never made
one mistake'''

"But I've never done
anything either!"

IN A NUTSHELL

Mistakes are not really mistakes. Let's expect to make some errors in judgement and welcome them as part of the learning process. Also, if we don't take ourselves too seriously, it is a whole lot easier to live with a few mistakes. The shame is never in having failed — the shame is only in not having tried.

THE LAW OF SOW AND REAP

"Success is simply a matter of luck. Ask any failure!"
Earl Wilson.

Newton discovered the law of cause and effect: in other words that for every action there is an equal and opposite reaction. We only get back if we put out. If we plant tomatoes, we don't reap thistles. It is important to remind ourselves that this principle affects everything we do and every experience we have.

We can't beat the law. Our physical health, our mental health, our business success and our personal relationships are each governed by the same equation which requires us to "pay up front". The fascinating thing about the law is that we never know quite when we will be rewarded; when we will receive the dividends on our time and effort. But the rewards always come and the uncertainty of their time of arrival only serves to make life more exciting.

In addition, what we have in our life at the moment is a result of the sowing we have been doing until now. If we currently enjoy warm friendships and loving relationships, it is because we have prepared the ground and planted the seed. If our business is currently flowering, it is because we've expended the effort to get the results.

If we talk about others, we'll be talked about. If we speak well of others, they will speak well of us. If we rip people off then we will be ripped off. If we rejoice in the success of others, we will be more likely to enjoy success ourselves. If we tell lies, we will be told lies. If we criticize, we will be criticized. If we love, we will in turn receive love.

Historically, we can see the Golden Rule has been expressed in many different ways and the principle is constant — "you will be treated by others as you treated them. You will get back what you put in."

On an Egyptian tomb dating back to 1600 B.C., are written the "words": "He sought for others the good he desired for himself."

Confucius said, "What you would not want done to yourself, do not do to others."

Aristotle said. "We should behave to the world as we wish the world to behave towards us."

In the Bible we read, "Do unto others as you would have others do unto you."

These principles apply to our relationships and they apply equally to what we reap in the other dimensions of life. James Allen, in his book, "As a Man Thinketh", put it beautifully when he wrote —

"Every man is where he is by the law of his being; the thoughts which he has built into his character have brought him there, and in the arrangement of his life there is no element of chance, but all

result of a law which cannot err.

Man is buffeted by circumstances so long as he believes himself to be the creature of outside conditions, but when he realises that he is a creative power, and that he may command the hidden soil and seeds of his being out of which his circumstances grow, he then becomes the rightful master of himself.

That circumstances grow out of thought every man knows who has for any length of time practiced self-control and self-purification, for he will notice that the alteration in his circumstances has been in exact ratio with his altered mental condition".

The ignorant will often stand by observing those who are outstanding and remark, "I wish I had his talent!" or "I wish I had her luck", and they never see the months and years of effort that molded that·person's success. How often do we read about the "overnight success" in show business and find that this new superstar has actually been slogging away for fifteen years!

The wonderful thing about nature is that it gives us back much more than we put out. When you plant a pumpkin seed, you don't just get back one seed! Otherwise, why bother? Nature is very generous. Plant a few seeds and you may end up with a truckload of pumpkins. Again, this principle works with everything we do, but first we need to get out in the fields and dig!

IN A NUTSHELL

The universe is fair and just. We get back from life only what we put into it.

RISK

"It costs so much to be a full human being that there are very few who have the love and courage to pay the price. One has to abandon altogether the search for security and reach out to the risk of living with both arms. One has to embrace life like a lover".

Morris West.

To achieve any goal, there is always risk involved. Fred may say, "Well, I'm not taking any risks. I'm not going out on a limb!" What Fred doesn't realize is that out on the limb is where the fruit is. That is where the fruit has always been — out on the limb. There is a law working on this planet which ensures that the rewards come after the risk, and not the other way around.

Most of us start out our lives with a healthy attitude toward risk. As children we can't wait to try new adventures. Hence, mothers, invariably find their two-year-olds on the tops of ladders, strolling down the highway, on the roof, pulling horses tails and suchlike. A healthy, happy child, like a healthy happy adult, loves to test and stretch himself. When we take those first faltering steps, as we begin to master the art of walking, we are taking risks. And we love it!

Somehow between the age of two and the age of twenty-two, many people undergo a dramatic change of attitude. They become preoccupied with being "safe and secure". They spend their nights glued to the television, spellbound by the daring exploits of celluloid superheroes. They shoot up on large doses of "soap" and situation comedy, while their own lives degenerate into a parade of one boring year after the next.

The spice of life is in doing new things, in forging something from our own substance. The search for safety and security stifles our life force. The ultimate in being safe and secure, and free of all worries, is in lying in a box, six feet under.

In loving and caring, we risk. Telling another person "I love you", can be a risky business, but the rewards can be fantastic. Being different is risky, and it also means that you can be yourself. The dangerous and difficult occupations are well rewarded. In fact, the universe is continually encouraging us to stretch, to climb, to be extraordinary.

To gain, we must risk. To learn to walk, we must risk falling over and getting hurt. To make a dollar, we must risk losing it, and the people who make the most, risk the most. To have a chance of winning a game of tennis, we face the possibility of losing.

Winners take more risks than losers. That is why they win so much. Necessarily then, winners lose more than losers, but they are playing so often that their wins add up — and we remember the winners for their victories, not their failures. We remember Edison for his lightbulb that worked, not for the truckload of bulbs that didn't.

IN A NUTSHELL

We have a choice. It is the choice between really living, or merely existing. Getting a job is a risk. Crossing the road is a risk. Starting a business, a relationship or a family is a risk. Eating in a restaurant is a risk. (Some are more risky than others!) Life is a risk. So let's get out on some limbs and pick some fruit.

COMMITMENT

"Until one is committed
there is hesitancy, the chance to draw back,
always ineffectiveness.
Concerning all acts of initiative (and creation)
there is one elementary truth,
the ignorance of which kills countless ideas
and splendid plans:
that the moment one definitely commits oneself,
then Providence moves too.
All sorts of things occur to help one
that would otherwise never have occurred.
A whole stream of events issues from the decision,
raising in one's favor all manner
of unforeseen incidents and meetings
and material assistance,
which no man could have dreamt
would have come his way.

　　　W. N. Murray

Whatever you can do, or dream you can . . . begin it. Boldness has genius, power and magic in it."

Goethe

We have to make the first move. As long as we stand around on the edge of things, unprepared to jump in, the universe seems to take the attitude, "Well, you don't seem very serious about this. Once you're committed, then you'll get some help."

The moment we declare, "I'll do this thing, no matter what!" we somehow tap into that "genius, power and magic".

Everybody who achieves in life, makes decisions to do so. The mountain climber who conquers Mt. Everest is the one who says "I WILL do it." Those who proclaim, "I'll give it my best shot", or "I'll have a go" or "I'll try" will likely come home early. The same goes for the business person, the sports person, the husband or the wife. We need to get serious to get results.

Gandhi's life was testimony to the fact that one person, totally committed, could change the course of a nation's history. Disraeli put it well when he said, "Nothing can resist the human will that will stake even its existence on the extent of its purpose."

It is best that we also realize that whenever we make a stand on something, people will test us out. Children are always doing it with their parents; testing and testing and secretly hoping that their parents will stand firm.

People are always looking for someone to admire. Although your brother-in-law may say, "Are you finished with this crazy scheme of yours yet?" and although your neighbor may tempt you with chocolate cream cakes five minutes after you announce the start of your new diet, they are each secretly hoping that you will have the strength to stand by your commitment.

In addition, an interesting thing happens when we commit ourselves. Often, the commitment is enough. In other words, if you are prepared to do anything to achieve your goal, generally you won't have to. But if you are only half serious, you may well be tested to the limit!

IN A NUTSHELL

One person said it this way, "Here's how to get whatever you want — do whatever it takes!"

EFFORT

"There aint no such thing as a free lunch!"

Insects and animals are nearly always busy; preparing for winter, getting ready for spring, washing themselves, cleaning their nests, feeding their young and doing the things that animals and insects do. They are a hundred percent alive and involved. They also appear to be particularly content.

We can learn from animals. To be happy we need to be industrious. When we let things slide, it costs us. Things don't improve where we neglect them: sailors know this about boats, athletes know it about their bodies, students know it about their minds, we all know it about the state of our garage. Any gardener finds out early that weeds come up automatically. You don't have to plant a single weed to have undergrowth right across your backyard. Things only improve with effort.

Our attitude to effort is important.

We need to put in the effort because we WANT to do it; because it is our privilege and joy to learn, to test ourselves, to experiment and experience. The mistake that many people make is to work only for end results and not for the joy of working. Then, if they don't get the results they want, they are disappointed.

A salesman may make the phone calls and make no sales, and so decide that he has had a bad day. No! He needs to make the calls because he wants to make the calls. He needs to delight in his own ability to experience new things, to refine his skills and rejoice in his capacity to persevere. If he can adopt the attitude, "Well, I'll enjoy what I'm doing for the sake of doing it. I'll experience my own aliveness while I'm doing it and focus my full attention on my task," then any results will be a bonus.

Emerson said, "The reward of a thing well done is to have done it." Getting too hung up on results takes us out of the present moment. It is possible to be always focusing on what is ahead and not on what we are doing. This approach removes us from the enjoyment of the present moment. As we detach ourselves a little from the results, we can enjoy what we are doing for the sake of it.

Let us say that you are at your mother-in-law's house and you decide to wash her car as a surprise. One approach is to spend the whole time thinking, "I'm really getting wet out here and she had better appreciate this and thank me profusely or I'll be very irritated." That is a

loser's attitude. The alternative approach is to say, "I'm going to enjoy this car washing because I'm in control of my own mind and if I want to enjoy it, I will. I will see how quickly and efficiently I can get the job done." Now, if your mother-in-law showers praise upon you for your services, that's nice — a bonus. If she doesn't, that is fine too. You have enjoyed it anyway.

If we work for the love of working, of being involved, then there is no problem. Results will always come. They necessarily must. It is a law. However, if the results are delayed or don't come when you expect them, you don't let it wreck your whole week (or year). Results always come.

And how do you work for the love of working? Decide to. It is like being happy. It is a decision. As James M. Barrie said, "The secret of being happy is not in doing what one likes, but in liking what one does."

IN A NUTSHELL

The story of Fritz Kreisler, the great violinist illustrates beautifully the relation between effort and success. After a virtuoso performance, he was approached by a woman who said, "Mr. Kreisler, I would give my life to play as you have!"

He smiled at the woman and said, "I did!"

When we change, things change .

A lot of people spend their whole life hoping that things will get better. They wish that everything was easier, and seem to hope that one day a magic wand will come down and sort out their mess. No way!

Things get better as we get better. Things change when we change and not before. James Rohn, the American multi-millionaire businessman, says in his seminars, "Unless you change how you are, you will always have what you've got!" He says, "If someone hands you a million dollars, best you become a millionaire or you won't get to keep the money!" We need to put in the effort and develop the expertise and the self-image which go along with having that kind of wealth, or we may find ingenious ways of "redistributing" our assets.

What we have in our life stems from what we are. Surveys show that the majority of people who win huge sums of money in lotteries, manage to return to their previous struggling financial situations in record time. Two years after a big win, four out of five people are in a worse financial state than before their windfall. They haven't changed "inside" and so their outside situation has come to reflect the inside.

There is no way around it. For things to get better, we have to get better. Today will be much like yesterday unless we put in that effort.

PUT ALL YOU HAVE INTO ALL YOU DO

If you put all you have into whatever you do, you won't eliminate failure. If you put everything you have got into everything you do, you won't eliminate disappointment. So why bother?

The answer is, "For your own self-respect."

When your personal philosophy is, "I will do my best, regardless," you will always stand tall in your own estimation.

IN A NUTSHELL

Losing hurts, but it hurts even more when you realize that you haven't done your best.

"Superman, where are you?"

ELEVENTH HOURS

n seeking goals, it is important to know about these "eleventh hours."

Have you ever noticed in life that things can look really bleak just before a dramatic turn for the better? The businessman reports that just before he made his fortune, he was about to quit. He was up the creek without a paddle when, suddenly, everything began to fall into place. He hung in there just long enough to reap his rewards.

We read about the sporting champion who was down and out and couldn't win a match. On the verge of giving in, he stayed just long enough to turn his career around and reap the glory.

Perhaps you have had the experience, when wondering if life was worth all the effort, you met somebody who lifted you into the clouds.

Life is like that because there is a principle at work here — the "eleventh hour" principle. It is always darkest and coldest just before dawn. But if we hang on long enough, we will get our rewards.

If we look at childbirth we see the principle in evidence also. Just before the most incredible gift of life, the mother-to-be has her patience truly tested and undergoes considerable pain and anguish. (My mother tells me it was all worth it!)

Once we recognize the eleventh hour for what it is, life loses a lot of its trauma. In effect, the universe often seems to be testing us to see if we are serious about attaining our goal. If we hang on that little bit longer . . . Bingo!

Once we realize what is happening, we can actually be one step ahead. When everything looks bleak, we can then tell ourselves, "So everything is going wrong! This could mean that everything that I have been striving for is just around the corner." Then we should feel better.

We will generally be tested in some way before achieving something of value. If we can pick the eleventh hour for what it is; and treat any difficulties as a necessary part of the process of achievement, then, firstly we won't be quitters, and secondly, we will achieve whatever we desire in life.

IN A NUTSHELL

Don't be fooled. The eleventh hour is usually an impostor. When everything looks black, it could be time to celebrate. You may be nearly home.

PERSISTENCE

"Nothing in the world can take the place of persistence. Talent will not; nothing is more common than unsuccessful men with talent. Genius will not; unrewarded genius is almost a proverb. Education will not; the world is full of educated derelicts. Persistence and determination alone are omnipotent. The slogan "Press on" has solved and always will solve the problems of the human race."

Calvin Coolidge.

Persistence is a secret. Successful people know the secret — they realize that it is the main ingredient in winning at anything. Failures tend to view persistence as some kind of "optional extra."

Most people quit. Wherever we look, we see mostly quitters. The average person who starts learning to play a musical instrument, quits. How many people do you know who play a "little piano" or a few chords on the guitar? They tried it for a while, results came too slowly, so they quit, and went to look for something easier.

The average person who goes to oil painting classes, quits. The average individual who starts out selling life insurance, quits. (In fact, about ninety eight people out of every hundred quit in the first year!). For that matter, most people who try any kind of selling, quit.

Many people who start university, quit. At the beginning of the year there is standing room only. By the end of the year, there is room to park a truck in the classroom! Most people who start a fitness program, quit. People who start savings plans, quit. People who set out to write books, quit.

Most people are quitters. This is wonderful news for those of us who decide to be successful. It means that if we stick to what we are doing, we will, in a very short time, be ahead of the multitudes. As the saying goes, "A big shot is simply a little shot that kept shooting!"

Edison produced thousands of inventions including light bulbs, gramophones and the Universal Stock ticker. His influence on this planet has been absolutely enormous. It is too easy to envy his creative genius and discount his extraordinary commitment to his projects.

He said, "Genius is one percent inspiration and ninety nine percent perspiration . . . I never did anything worth doing by accident, nor did any of my inventions come by accident. They came by work."

Michelangelo, one of the greatest painters and sculptors who ever lived, once commented, "If people knew how hard I have had to work to gain my mastery, it wouldn't seem wonderful at all."

History is dotted with classic examples of persistence. The chicken man, Colonel Sanders, peddled his then not very famous recipe in and out of one thousand and nine restaurants and food outlets until he finally found some interest. His eventual success proved the value of a little "Kentucky Fried Persistence."

At the age of twenty, Julio Iglesias had a car accident which left him crippled from the waist down. It appeared that he would spend his life in a wheelchair, but Julio refused to accept that possibility. He practiced twelve hours a day for two months, just to be able to move his little toe. Bit by bit, over a period of nearly two years, he regained the use of his lower limbs. He would drag himself by his arms up and down the hallway of his parents' home, hoping that his legs would somehow get the idea that they should start working again.

He had mirrors installed along the length of the hallway so he could motivate himself as he dragged himself about. In the end, the same determination and commitment to excellence which rebuilt his body, built his career as an international recording phenomenon.

Recall for a moment, the times when you have watched quitters in action — on the tennis court, in a card game, in business, in relationships. Mostly, it is no fun quitting and it's no fun watching quitters.

Of course, there are times when quitting is the smartest move — if the ship is sinking, it is time to get off. We should not mistake stubbornness for persistence! If you hate the job, dislike where you live, or see better opportunities elsewhere, sometimes the solution is to get out.

The problem is that for many, quitting becomes a habit — a "persistent" pattern.

IN A NUTSHELL

For every OUTSTANDING achievement, persistence is a common ingredient. The name of the game is persistence.

ASK

"Ask and ye shall receive"

Lesson number one in how to get what you want . . . ASK for it! Have you ever said to somebody, "I don't mind doing things for people, but I can't bear asking them to do something for me?" Is it not ironic that, in a world where many despair that they never get back from life all they would like, most people won't ask for it?

It is important that we ask for what we want for four reasons —

1. ASKING INDICATES SELF-WORTH AND SELF-ESTEEM. Asking confirms in our own mind and in the minds of others that we have rights and privileges. It means you feel you deserve and it starts to create an attitude of expectancy.

2. ASKING IS IMPORTANT FOR YOUR HEALTH. When you don't ask, you can be overlooked, ignored, left out. That leads to frustration, knots in your gut and so on. Whenever you don't express yourself, your stomach keeps count.

3. ASKING IS THE FIRST LOGICAL STEP TO TAKE IN LETTING GOD, YOUR BOSS, YOUR FAMILY AND FRIENDS KNOW WHAT YOU

WANT. Most of the aforementioned parties aren't mind-readers!

4. ASKING GIVES SOMEBODY ELSE THE PLEASURE OF HELPING YOU. In fact, FAILING TO ASK IS SELFISH. If you like to help others, then give them the same opportunity. Don't deprive them of the satisfaction of helping you!

This applies to all kinds of asking. People for the most part are more than willing to help if they perceive that you are in need or if they believe that you are already doing everything you can, and that you need some extra assistance. Many people are DESPERATE to help, but fear they may impose.

Women have told me that, when they have been obviously pregnant, strangers have become wonderfully thoughtful and caring, way beyond the "call of duty." People really want to help. They are at least fairly confident that their efforts to help a pregnant lady onto a bus or into a car, won't be rejected. Generally, they are less confident that their thoughtfulness will be as gratefully received by those of us who are "unpregnant."

Maybe you know people who continually seem to fall on their feet in their business and personal lives. Whether they are buying cars or seeking employment or doing deals or getting married, they manage to get just the results that they are after. They do it by asking for what they want.

Recently I had some friends visit me. They all wanted to go out to dinner at a particular seafood restaurant. The restaurant of course was full . . . until my friend Peter did some asking. His conversation, the side that we heard, went like this;

"So you are really full?"

"Is that really, really, full?"

"I see. We have just come over from interstate and we are hoping that we can eat at your restaurant tonight. There're only six of us."

"That full, huh?"

"If you did have a space for us, where would you put us?"

"Yes, but if you did?"

"That full!"

"What seems to be the major problem? Is it a shortage of tables or chairs?"

"Well, could you check?"

"Thank you."

"So, it is chairs you are short of. Well, we just happen to have six spare chairs right here. How would it be if we brought our own?"

"You'll have to check with the manager? Sure, I can wait."

"Eight thirty will be perfect. Thank you very much. We will see you then."

Peter ate at the restaurant of his choice that night because he was prepared to ask some questions. He was always friendly and polite. He simply asked for what he wanted. (The rest of us ate at the restaurant of our choice because we asked Peter to make the phone call!).

The issue, though, is not about getting into your favorite restaurant. It is about realizing that it is OK to ask anybody for what you want. Ask for a ride to work when your car is with the mechanic. Ask the passenger next to you in the plane not to smoke when you are eating your breakfast. (Be subtle about asking him to step outside to light up!). Ask if you can go to work for whomever it is that you would dearly love to work.

I am not advocating that we become sponges and freeloaders. I am saying that asking gives you information and gives other people the opportunity to help you if it suits them. Surprisingly often it does suit them! A survey of successful people would reveal that they are more able to ask when they want something done.

Sometimes people say no.

What if fifty percent of the time you asked, the other person said, "No!". Would that mean you are a nasty person? Would that mean that you are undeserving? No! It would mean that half the time your ideas didn't mesh with someone else's plans. It would also mean that the other fifty percent of the time you had a lot of help that you otherwise would not have had.

In asking for what you want, you are also helping in the personal development of the person to whom the request is made! How? If they choose to help you, they will benefit from the experience. If they don't choose to help you, they will also benefit because an important part of being an effective individual is being able to say no without guilt. You can now start giving a lot more people practice at this!

Additionally, from your point of view, when you are an "asker", you take more responsibility for your life. There is less danger of you becoming one of those silent sufferers who soldier on gamely, doing it all themselves because that is the way martyrs do it.

Mind you, some people prefer to be martyrs. They have developed their suffering into an art form, and woe betide anyone who seeks to make their path any easier. We should also respect their right to live their life the way they choose.

IN A NUTSHELL

A major ingredient in you getting what you want is having the conviction that you are worth it. When you both subconsciously and consciously have that sense of worth, you will have more of your needs and wants met. One of the best ways to develop your sense of worth is to ASK.

REASONS OR RESULTS

The bottom line is always "Are you happy doing what you are doing?"

Let's take a fellow who is in a job he hates, earning less than he wants, missing out on the holidays and trips that he would love to take, he is lonely, depressed, he has never learned the skills he would dearly love to learn and has never done the things he said he wanted to do with his short stay on this planet.

But he has got all these great reasons for why he is where he is! He has a mental list. He blames the government, he blames his wife, he blames his kids, he blames his star sign, he blames his boss, the economy, he blames his bad back and his bad luck and his lack of education and his brother-in-law. And there is more!

Somehow he arrived at the idea that if you have enough excuses and things to blame, it is OK to be miserable. NO! NO! NO! It is not OK; in life we have either reasons or results. Some people get the idea that they both weigh the same. They don't.

You can have a list as long as your arm. You can have a list as long as your street. It does not count for anything. Nothing! If you are not living the life you want to live, doing the things you really want to do, no excuse is any compensation.

When we take a look around, we can find all kinds of people beating the odds. We see people achieving and being happy with no education, people making money in the current economic climate, people leading exciting

REASONS WHY
I AM MISERABLE.
I BLAME
• MY EDUCATION
• THE GOVERNMENT
• MY HEALTH
• MY NEIGHBORS
(THEY HATE ME)
• MY WIFE (SHE
DRIVES ME NUTS)
• THE KIDS
• THE MORTGAGE
• MY PARENTS
• MY JOB
• EVERYBODY (THEY
DON'T UNDERSTAND
ME).

I BLAME YOU

happy lives with their eight children, people who have lifted their marriages from the ashes and fallen back in love. These are the people who are demonstrating to us that results are the only things which matter. These are the individuals who have made the same discovery as the man who said, "I used to blame the weather; and then I found out it rains on rich people too!"

The enjoyment we derive from life is inversely proportional to how much we blame our circumstances.

IN A NUTSHELL

You have but one life to lead. If you go to your grave with a list of "reasons why I didn't" as long as your street, all it means is that YOU DIDN'T.

LEARNING FROM NATURE

Music is the space between the notes . . .

NATURAL LAWS

There are laws and principles of the universe affecting our lives every minute of the day. For example, we are generally aware of the law of gravity. If you lose your grip on a bag of potatoes and it falls on your big toe, you are soon reminded of the law. We also observe what gravity does to old houses and old people; they sag and sometimes fall down. We also accept that laws govern the orbiting of the planets, the cycle of the tides and the changes of the seasons.

*"Unless I see it,
I don't believe it!"*

If we poke our fingers into a light socket we become particularly aware of electricity. We may not see it but there is strong evidence to suggest its existence. Magnetism is a similar story in that we accept it although we don't see it. Principles which are invisible help to shape our lives.

The remarkable thing is that many people believe that everything in the universe is governed by law except when it comes to their own lives and their own success or lack of it, and then they talk of fate, chance and "the breaks". Well, you are a part of the universe and your life is governed by laws as absolutely as are the moon and the stars and the weeds in your front garden. And you are a cause of what happens in your life. You are a cause by your own thoughts.

What is a thought?

Physicists tell us that the world isn't really the way it looks. When we break down the material world around us into its smallest "building blocks", we get atoms and sub-atomic particles. These pieces of matter, vibrating at enormous speed are actually packets of energy. The material world is made of energy. Nothing is really solid, and the speed of the vibration of these packets of energy determines whether a "piece of stuff" is a brick or a blob of toothpaste. In simple terms, the solid material world you think you know is actually a mass of energies vibrating at various speeds.

Guess what your brain produces when you have a thought? Energy! Vibrations. Now science tells us that for every action there is an equal and opposite reaction. So for every time you produce a thought, with its own unique vibration, you must be producing a reaction or consequence. As you may have around fifty thousand thoughts a day, you're sending out a lot of vibrations and producing a lot of consequences. What I wish to establish here is that thoughts are real forces. We're dealing with energy.

Plato spoke of these forces when he said, "Reality is created by the mind. We can change our reality by changing our mind." The Roman, Marcus Aurelius, wrote "A man's life is what his thoughts make of it." The Bible said, "Man is what he thinks about all day long." Throughout history, those people with awareness have spoken of the power of the mind.

(Incidentally, this book quotes the words and writings of many perceptive people. We are well served by learning from other people's learning. We have the choice in life of heeding the advice of winners or listening to losers. I recommend the former and believe that the philosophy and understanding of successful people is a principal ingredient in their success).

In dealing with these universal principles, I concede that sometimes there appear to be exceptions to the rule. Nevertheless, I suggest that there is an order about this complex spinning planet and that having some awareness of the laws at work will make our stay here a smoother and happier one.

There will always be those people who say, "Nothing works, nothing matters, nothing makes any difference and life stinks!" Let's first assess the quality of their lives before we are sold on their plan! During my lecturing in the field of personal development, I sometimes encounter the attitude, "I know none of this stuff works because I've never tried it." Use the ideas expressed in this book and then make up your own mind.

Many of the concepts in this book won't be new to you. For ideas that tend to stretch your belief system, I hope that you will approach them with an open mind and open yourself to the possibility that there may be things about the universe that you haven't fully figured out yet. As a child you probably once thought that the earth was flat. When you received more information on the subject you may have been prepared to change your ideas. This is the spirit in which I hope you will embrace the concepts herein. Don't believe anything because it is written here. Make your own assessment.

LEARNING FROM NATURE

"You are a part of the universe, no less than the stars and trees, and you have a right to be here. And whether it is clear to you or not, no doubt the universe is unfolding as it should . . ."

Desiderata

We are part of the universe and our lives are governed by the same laws that govern the rest of the cosmos. We need to keep a balance as does the rest of nature. We take time to grow and time to heal. Our lives will always move in cycles because that is the universal law. We need time to rest and recuperate, as do all other living things.

TAKING TIME

Nature always takes her time. Great oaks don't become great overnight. They also lose a lot of leaves, branches and bark in the process of becoming great. Diamonds aren't formed in a week either. Everything of value, of beauty, of majesty in the universe took time to become so.

So it will be with our own growth and development. Let us recognize the way things work down here, and so be gentler on ourselves when assessing our own progress. It takes time to build confidence, to build a healthy body or a positive outlook. It takes time to build a business of value or to create our own financial independence. In the real world there are very few instant, overnight successes.

CYCLES

As sure as the earth revolves around the sun and winter follows the spring, so must our life move in cycles. So there will always be easy times and there will be hard times, as sure as one season follows another. One of the great challenges of life is dealing with the winter while you are waiting for things to get better.

Things will get better. They always do. The trouble is that many people give up and go home too early. The tide will always turn.

REST

Nature has a rest from time to time. The soil needs a rest, bears and snakes hibernate; even fish sleep with their eyes open. We can learn from this approach. We need to take time out; to rest, to review, to ponder, to be.

If you decide that you are indispensable and that you must always have your nose to the grindstone, then you can live your life like that. Your belief that you can never rest will be your reality until such time as you decide differently.

When we do make rest a part of our lifestyle, like the soil we become so much more productive when we work. Having said this, I believe that as humans we are engineered for enterprise and activity. Rohn says, "Make rest a necessity, not an objective!"

LOVE

few thoughts on love . . . (How does one do justice to love in a few paragraphs?).

Have you ever wondered why we love babies so much? We like babies because they are so open and vulnerable. As they open their arms and look into our eyes, they say to us, "Love me. I need you and I can't make it all alone."

As we grow older, many of us come to believe that we have to fake self-sufficiency. We pretend. We say, "I'm all right, I'm OK, I'm tough, I can handle it", while inside we may be frightened, lonely and craving for someone to listen.

There is a myth around that says, "You had better not admit that you are vulnerable or lonely, or you will look weak." It also says, "Don't be honest about how you really feel, or someone will sink the boot in." The myth is back to front. Others know when we are being open and sincere and they love us for it. It is only when we fake it and pretend that we are OK, that we get into trouble.

It is ironic that those of us who are the most desperate for affection, do the most pretending that we don't need it. When we are really soft and lonely inside, we then have to do an extra good job of letting the world know that everything is fine.

Love is not ooey gooey. Love is strength and commitment. To love someone can mean telling them what they don't want to hear.

Love is courage, and it takes a lot more courage to say "I'm scared," or "I love you," than it does to clout someone around the ears.

Love is respect, for ourselves and others. It is all about allowing people to be where they are and loving them anyway. The moment we say, you do this and then I will love you, that isn't love — it is manipulation.

Love is about looking for the good in people, and if we can do that, and do it consistently, then our own happiness is guaranteed. As our life is a reflection of ourselves, the more love and beauty that we perceive, the more we are growing and the more we are becoming, and so for all of us, LOVE IS EVERYTHING.

LEARNING FROM CHILDREN

We can learn so much from children. And most of us have the good fortune to get to be closely reacquainted with the magic of childhood twenty or thirty years after we were children. If our children then have children, we get another lesson some years further down the track.

It would seem that many parents see the teaching process as a one way street. I believe that they would do well to spend more time learning from their children and less time teaching.

Children know a lot more about having a good time than most adults. Children know how to laugh. They don't need much to laugh at.

Sometimes they don't need anything at all. They laugh because it feels good. Did you get your quota of laughs today?

They are delightfully spontaneous. Children don't analyze and work everything out. They just are, busy "being". Whenever we meet grown ups who are so spontaneous, we tend to treasure them also. Let's do less thinking and more responding.

Children are eternally fascinated. They are curious. A rock or a beetle or puddle or a mouse is a source of wonderment to a child. Everything is a new and exciting experience, to be absorbed. Adults switch off. They don't really know any more about rocks and beetles, puddles and mice. There is still lots for all of us to know about these things, but the trouble is that by the time we have reached adulthood, many of us have forgotten what a magic place this planet is.

Children are also very accepting. They are without prejudice. Rich or poor or black or white, you are O K. A child is not fussed by your religion or your politics. Children don't even care much whether you bathe or not. They accept you. They accept circumstances until they learn not to. How often do you hear young children complain about the weather? They don't. They intuitively know that in order to maintain mental health, you have to go with the flow.

Haven't we all been stunned and delighted by children's honesty? "How come you look so old?" "Are you going to die soon?" "Why are you thumping the table?" "Johnny's father smiles. Why don't you?"

Kids have enormous resilience and determination. If they want something, they don't quit. So we hear, "Can I have an ice cream?" "I want an ice cream." "Johnny gets ice creams." Their persistence is really something to be admired, as well as endured. If insurance salesmen did their training in a kindergarten, maybe ninety eight percent of them wouldn't quit in the first twelve months! Children just keep on going for it. When you learned to walk, you kept at it and kept at it. You fell over and got up. You fell on your face and got up again. Finally you learned to walk! Do you still exhibit that kind of determination?

As I said earlier, children have an enormous imagination. It enables them to learn and to retain and develop so quickly.

IN A NUTSHELL

Spend time with children. Learn more about laughter, spontaneity, curiosity, acceptance, resilience, trust, determination, and your imagination. They are here to teach us!

KEEP MOVING

R elated to the "Use it or Lose it" law, is the "Keep Moving" principle. We learn about stagnation from nature. A river that stops moving gets putrid. The same thing happens to people who stop moving, either mentally or physically.

Those who play contact sports know that the player who usually gets hurt the most is the one who is standing still. People in business know the same thing: stand still for too long and you are finished. Of course you'll need some time to catch your breath every so often, but the essential message is, "keep moving, extending and learning".

Ships last a lot longer when they go to sea than when they stay in the harbor. The same is true for airplanes. You don't preserve an airplane

by keeping it on the ground. You preserve it by keeping it in service. We also get to live a long healthy life by staying "in service".

Longevity statistics reveal that the average person doesn't last very long after retirement. The moral here is, "Don't retire!" If a fellow says, "I am ninety four years old and I've worked all my life," we need to realize that is how he got to be ninety four. By staying involved.

George Bernard Shaw won a Nobel Prize when nearly seventy, Benjamin Franklin produced some of his best writings age eighty four and Pablo Picasso put brush to canvas right through his eighties. Isn't the issue how old we think we are?

I know a lady in Adelaide, South Australia, who had never played a sport in her life. She started a badminton club for over sixties when she was seventy six years old! She is now eighty two, and still playing twice a week.

A bonus with the keep moving principle is that while we keep moving, we don't have a chance to worry. Hence we avoid the dreaded "paralysis by analysis".

IN A NUTSHELL

There is happiness and fulfillment in activity. The "Keep Moving" principle is continually encouraging us to get off our backsides and to get involved.

USE IT OR LOSE IT

Whatever we don't use, we lose. It is particularly easy to see this principle at work in our physical bodies. If you decide to spend three years in a wheelchair for no other reason except that you like sitting down, when the three years are up, you won't be able to walk. Stop using your legs and they stop working.

The same applies to any skill. If you stop playing the piano for twelve months, you lose your touch. Stop using your creative imagination and it will evaporate. We are designed such that we need to, in fact, have to stay involved. Keep practicing the art of living.

In addition, when you practice extending yourself you become more courageous. Nobody gets to be courageous by locking himself in his bedroom, trying to save up his courage! We develop strength by regularly testing ourselves.

We need to keep caring. Our conscience can switch off the same as anything else. Once we start to say, "Nothing matters much", we are heading for trouble. Prison cells and mental hospitals are crammed full of people for whom things ceased to matter, people who have managed to switch off their feelings until there is nothing left. Things do matter.

We have to keep using our mind to keep it in shape. There is no reason why we should become less able as the years go by. If we keep on using our mental capacity to the full, our mind will keep on working for us.

This same principle applies to money. Money is meant to be used. It needs to circulate. People who make big money, keep reinvesting their capital, using what they have, taking risks. You don't become a millionaire by storing your pennies in a paper bag under the bed!

IN A NUTSHELL

The universe is continually encouraging us to stay involved. The law of use is wonderful! It gives us the incentive to practice, and as we practice we get better. Use it or lose it. Unless we continue to make the most of all that we have, we don't get to keep it.

RELAX AND LET GO (GO WITH THE FLOW)

Have you noticed what happens when you are trying really, really hard to remember something or to hit a tennis ball just right or solve a problem? Invariably, you don't get the results you want.

In their search for ideas and solutions to problems, most people note that they have their greatest success while they are engaged in activities where they are naturally relaxed. Hence they have their brainwaves in the shower, in the bath, in bed, in the toilet: places where we relax easily.

To understand the scientific angle, when we relax, our brain rhythms move into a slower mode — the alpha mode — where we are far more able and creative. Results come easily. When you step into a warm shower, you naturally relax. In bed, the same happens; and so you will find you get ideas in bed! You can be very creative in the bedroom. You are open to ideas in the toilet, because you have to relax in there just to get the job done!

Of course, physical relaxation is equally important for peak performance. As we relax our physical body, our whole metabolism comes into balance; our blood pressure drops, our breathing becomes deep and easy, and the organs in our system work harmoniously.

On a broader scale, the same picture emerges. We got the best results in our life when we are prepared to go with the flow. This means finding the delicate and elusive balance between effort and relaxation, between attachment and letting go. It is no simple thing to achieve!

Again, we can take our lead from nature. The birds and the animals work, but they don't work day and night. They know when they have had enough. Try talking a sparrow into a little nightshift! Sparrows know when it's time to have a break. So do bears and frogs and reindeer and possums. Animals know lots of things that we only half know.

Even the soil needs a rest every so often. That one gets us into trouble too! We plant beans on the same plot for twenty three consecutive years, we cram the earth with chemicals to keep them popping up, and wonder why the beans taste worse than the fertilizer. Everything needs a rest. Everything takes time to regenerate, to have an ebb and flow.

Benjamin Hoff wrote a delightful book, "The Tao of Pooh," in which he expounds the Eastern philosophy of "Tao", as intuitively applied by Pooh, the all time favorite "bear of little brain". He suggests that we can learn much from Winnie the Pooh's easy, accepting, uncomplicated philosophy — "while Eyeore frets, and Piglet hesitates and Owl pontificates . . . Pooh just IS."

Hoff writes:

"When we learn to work with our own Inner Nature, and with the natural laws operating around us, we reach the level of Wu Wei. Then we work with the natural order of things and operate on the principle of minimal effort. Since the natural world follows that principle, it does not make mistakes. Mistakes are made — or imagined — by man, the creature with the overloaded Brain who separates himself from the supporting network of natural laws by interfering and trying too hard."

We love Pooh because he doesn't try too hard. He lives in the present moment. He just is.

UNATTACHMENT

Our happiness and our free self-expression is much more assured if we let go of end results; work toward our goals and not be imprisoned by them.

We love the people who are least concerned about making an impression. They let go of any desperation for affection, so they automatically have the affection.

People who make a lot of money, only start to make it when they stop working for it! In other words, they find something they love to do and the wealth flows automatically. They have money because they let go of it. An outsider might say of someone who is financially successful, "The greedy pig. He is worth ten million dollars and he is still working!"

The man is working because he loves the challenge more than the money. That is why he is rich!

In a sense we need to be able to live without something in order to have it. Once we can let go, we are in a position of greater power. Successful businessmen know that the only way to pull off a successful deal is to "release" the deal — to become emotionally unattached.

Once we have done the work, it is time to let the results just happen in their own time. If you go out and plant your tomato crop, and then keep digging up the seeds every twenty minutes to see if they are doing their thing, it won't help! You need to relax a while. Let nature take its course.

IN A NUTSHELL

Going with the flow, taking time out, is as important as the activity itself. As Claude Debussy said, "Music is the space between the notes."

CHANGE

"Nothing endures but change."

Heraclitus.

T he Roman is reminding us that the law of the universe is change. Seasons come and seasons go. Nothing stays the same. This is basic, yet it seems we can forget the law sometimes and so suffer a lot of unnecessary disappointment and pain. We ask our lover, "Why can't you be like you were a year ago?" We take a vacation to the same place and lament, "It wasn't the same as last time!" Of course it wasn't! We buy some bread and groan, "It has gone up eight cents." Of course it has.

Things change. Life is dynamic. That is what makes it so beautiful and so unpredictable. The changes prod us into action.

The Buddhists say, "... all suffering of mankind is produced by attachment to a previous condition of existence." When we eliminate our expectations as to how the future ought to be a continuation of the past, we guarantee ourselves more peace of mind.

RELEASE

T hings being in a constant state of change, we need a healthy attitude toward letting go of old things and embracing the new. One thing is always replacing another. In getting rid of the old and the unnecessary, we create a vacuum and we draw to us new and exciting things.

When we hang on to the old and the outmoded, we create blocks, stagnation. This applies to habits, old clothes, junk in the closet, in the attic, in the garage and so on.

We must be prepared to let go of things. If you have loved people and you never actually let go of them in your mind, no one will come along to replace them. The minute you truly let go of those people and release them, and look toward new possibilities, you will have new relationships.

Our body can teach us lots about the value of elimination. It has no fewer than six ways aside from the skin as a whole, which it uses to get rid of unwanted material. What a disaster area we would be if our bodies never eliminated! From the same point of view, we need to eliminate mentally.

IN A NUTSHELL

To create a healthy flow, let go of all the stuff you don't want, won't use and don't need. Apart from feeling remarkably uplifted, you will find you are suddenly drawing new things to you like a magnet.

HOW MUCH DO WE REALLY UNDERSTAND

"If you think you understand everything that is going on, you are hopelessly confused."

Walter Mondale

Logically speaking, how do we attract into our life what we think about? How do we attract what we fear? Where do you actually find the subconscious and how do you explain its effect? If I think about health and imagine my body healthy, why does that make a difference? How can one explain the law of sow and reap? Why should my thoughts affect my prosperity?

Thus far we have touched on these principles and numerous others. Recognizing their existence and understanding how they work are two entirely different matters. We really don't know how they work! Science doesn't explain it. Science doesn't actually explain anything much at all!

Science describes what happens. Science puts labels on things. In grade school we begin to put names on things and if we are not careful, we might fool ourselves into thinking that we actually know what is happening on this planet. We have names like "instinct" and "magnetism" and "gravity" and "photosynthesis" which describe phenomena, but the bottom line is that we don't understand these things. The brilliant scientists and the enlightened scientists have always been more than happy to admit to this. As Einstein said, "The more I know, the more I realize I don't know."

You have spent your whole life working with principles and phenomena that you haven't understood! You don't really have a clue about how your digestive system works. Do you know how you digest a baked potato? No! You just eat it. Your inner mind takes care of the rest. What is it that stops you from suffocating on your pillow when you sleep at night? How does your mind manage to wake you up if you are actually asleep?

When you cut yourself, how do you manage to bond all the right cells back together? At what stage do you tell the scab to form, and then peel away? It all just happens — like magic! Does your bruised elbow heal any faster if you "know" all about histology and hemoglobin? No!

The fact is that all these things work for us and have done since we came into this world as lovely, little accepting bundles of joy. Isn't it wonderful?

Often, being rational and logical doesn't help us understand any more. On the surface it may appear to work, but at a much deeper level, a person runs out of intellectual explanations.

Science tells us that the universe is expanding at the speed of light. Well, assuming it is, what is it expanding into? Space that wasn't there already or space that was? Either way, just how logical is all this? Or, assuming that it isn't expanding, or even if it is, what is on the edge of this universe? A fence? How do you know when you get to the edge?

We can't even hope to begin to understand all the things which are happening around us and within us! We can't explain it all in logical terms. Most people happily agree with me on this point.

However, when I suggest to some people that their mind is like a magnet and that they attract circumstances, good or bad, as direct result of their positive or negative thinking, they say, "That's logical. Explain it."

We can't explain it!

Some people have difficulty believing that the creation of healthy pictures in their minds will directly influence the healing processes taking place in their bodies. They tend to say, "But how can I do that? I don't even know how my body works. I'm not a doctor!" You don't need to be a doctor to go to the toilet either! Isn't it wonderful the way things work?

Similarly, for some, it is difficult to believe that mental rehearsal dramatically improves performance. While they are trying to figure it out, others are using it to get results.

IN A NUTSHELL

If you decide that you want to understand everything before you use it, you could be waiting a long time — even for your next meal! Our mind is a miracle. Its ability to tap into all that is around us and produce results is truly beyond all comprehension.

There is enormous scope for heated argument and debate as to where our mind starts and God finishes or where God starts and our mind finishes or whether our mind really . . . These matters are not within the province of this book.

My experience has been that if we accept and use what we have, we do ourselves the most enormous favor. Let other people try and figure it all out. Let's go after the results.

LIFE IS WORTHLESS UNLESS YOU GIVE IT VALUE

"Nothing matters to the man who says nothing matters."
Lin Yutang

Life in itself has no value. Just because we are here does not mean that our lives have any value. Ultimately, only we decide whether our stay on this planet is to be our privilege and our joy, or whether it is to be a sentence of misery and despair.

If Fred is on the verge of suicide, and he says to us, "What is the point of it all? It is not worth the struggle!'', then that is Fred's reality, which he has created. And so his life is worth little.

There is not much we can do to change things for Fred. How do you get Fred excited about life if he does not want to jump for joy? You may be moved by walks along a sandy beach. You may be enthralled by that marvellous fluffy creation that is a kitten. You may thrill to the taste of avocados melting in your mouth. All these joys are available to Fred too but it is up to him to take it all in or not.

Ultimately we each make the decision as to whether we will focus on our awareness such that each walk in the country, each hot shower, each apple we eat, each conversation we have, each long ride we take, is a new experience, and not a replay of past events.

Life is not dull. There are only dull people who see their world through muddy, tainted glasses. Many people die at twenty five and don't get buried until they are seventy. It is a mystery to me why some people see beauty and magic everywhere they look, while others remain unmoved.

IN A NUTSHELL

However much beauty and magic you have enjoyed up until now, you can choose to have more from today. It is choice time, every day.

CHAPTER 6

TODAY IS IMPORTANT

Here Is Where You Begin

TODAY IS IMPORTANT

"A tree as big around as you can reach starts with a small seed; a thousand-mile journey starts with one small step."

Lao-tse.

You are where your thoughts and actions during the last few years have brought you. Whatever you will be experiencing in your next ten or twenty years will be influenced by what you do today. Your friends, your family, your job, your bank balance, where you will be living — all these things are being shaped by what you choose to do.

Life is a building process. What you do today affects what you will have tomorrow. Life doesn't happen in twenty four hour water tight compartments. Today's effort creates tomorrow's results. Whether you eliminate a nasty habit, whether you spend an hour with your family, whether you set some goals, whether you save or spend, whether you exercise your body, whether you stretch your mind — your decision makes the difference.

The ignorant never see it. Astute people know it. What we do today IS important.

You can get away with being casual and careless for a while but, sooner or later, things catch up with you. Leave your bills unpaid, your work undone and your problems to everyone else and you may manage for a month or so. Then one day the walls fall in and you wonder why there is no fun in your work, no money in the bank and nobody is very friendly any more. It is life reminding you that one day plus another has an accumulative effect.

IN A NUTSHELL

Wherever you are, it is the place to start. The effort you expend today does make a difference.

BIBLIOGRAPHY

ALLEN, James. As a Man Thinketh, DeVorss & Company, Marina del Rey, Ca.

BRISTOL, Claude M. 1948, The Magic of Believing, Pocket Books, New York.

BUSCAGLIA, Leo F. 1982, Loving, Living and Learning, Fawcett Columbine, New York.

COUSINS, Norman. 1979, The Anatomy of an Illness, W.W. Norton, New York.

DYER, Dr. Wayne, 1983, Gifts From Eykis, Pocket Books, New York.

GAWAIN, Shakti. 1978, Creative Visualization, Bantam Books, New York.

HARRISON, John, 1984, Love Your Disease, Angus and Robertson, London.

HILL, Napoleon. 1937, Think and Grow Rich, Wilshire Book Company, Hollywood.

HOFF, Benjamin. 1982, The Tao of Pooh, Methuen Children's Books Ltd., London.

LAUT, Phil. 1978, Money is my Friend, Trinity Publications, Hollywood, Ca.

MALTZ, Maxwell. 1960, Psycho-Cybernetics, Pocket Books, New York.

MURPHY, Joseph. 1963, The Power of Your Subconscious Mind, Prentice Hall, New Jersey.

ORR, Leonard and RAY, Sondra, 1977, Rebirthing in the New Age, Celestial Arts, Berkley, Ca.

OYLE, Dr. Irving. 1975, The Healing Mind, Celestial Arts, Millbrae, Ca.

RAY, Sondra. 1980, Loving Relationships, Celestial Arts, Berkley, Ca.

SCHINN, Florence Scovell. 1925, The Game of Life and How to Play It, DeVorss and Company, Marina del Rey, Ca.

WAITLEY, Denis. 1979, The Psychology of Winning, Nightingale–Conant Corporation, Chicago III.